Human Development

Human Development

Lessons from the Cuban Revolution

Henry Veltmeyer

Fernwood Publishing • Halifax & Winnipeg

Editing: Fran Slingerland
Cover design: John van der Woude
Printed and bound in Canada by Hignell Book Printing

Published by Fernwood Publishing
32 Oceanvista Lane, Black Point, Nova Scotia, B0J 1B0
and 748 Broadway Avenue, Winnipeg, Manitoba, R3G 0X3
www.fernwoodpublishing.ca

Fernwood Publishing Company Limited gratefully acknowledges the financial support
of the Government of Canada through the Canada Book Fund and the Canada Council
for the Arts, the Nova Scotia Department of Communities, Culture and Heritage,
the Manitoba Department of Culture, Heritage and Tourism under the
Manitoba Publishers Marketing Assistance Program and the Province of Manitoba,
through the Book Publishing Tax Credit, for our publishing program.

Library and Archives Canada Cataloguing in Publication

Veltmeyer, Henry, author
Human development: lessons from the Cuban revolution
/ Henry Veltmeyer.

Includes bibliographical references and index.
ISBN 978-1-55266-688-3 (pbk.)

1. Socialism—Cuba. 2. Quality of life—Cuba. 3. Cuba—Social
policy. 4. Cuba—Economic policy. I. Title.

HX158.5.V44 2014   303.44   C2014-902960-8

Contents

List of Acronyms and Terms

1968 Revolutionary Offensive – a policy adopted to abolish the market and the last vestiges of private enterprise in the Cuban economy

ALBA – Alianza Bolivariana para los Pueblos de Nuestra América – Bolivarian Alliance for the Peoples of Our America (until 2009, the name of this organization used the word Alternativa rather than Alianza). This alliance was founded by Cuba and Venezuela in 2004, and is named after Simón Bolívar (nineteenth-century leader who fought for democracy in South America and independence from colonial forces). ALBA is associated with socialist and social democratic governments wishing to consolidate regional economic integration based on a vision of social welfare, bartering and mutual economic aid. The member countries currently are Antigua and Barbuda, Bolivia, Cuba, Dominica, Ecuador, Nicaragua, Saint Vincent and the Grenadines, Venezuela and Saint Lucia.

ANAP – Asociación Nacional de Agricultores Pequeños – National Association of Smallhold Farmers

APP – Asambleas del Poder Popular – Assemblies of People's Power. This term refers to every grouping, from OLPPs, the Local Bodies of People's Power (see below), to People's Councils, the assemblies in neighbourhoods or workplaces, to the National Assembly, the legislative parliament of the Republic of Cuba.

campesinos – Cuban smallhold farmers prior to the revolution

CDR – Comités de Defensa de la Revolución – Committees for the Defence of the Revolution. Neighbourhood committees across Cuba described as the "eyes and ears of the Revolution." CDRs exist to promote social welfare and report on counter-revolutionary activity.

class consciousness – awareness of one's economic situation, formed in a process of a political struggle such as the Cuban Revolution

communalism – a political practice or ideology focused on the community or community-based local development

la conciencia (see also class consciousness) – an awareness on the part of a population — generated in the process of revolution — of cultural revolution and a socialist ethic

Consejos Populares – People's Councils, which were established in 1986 as a body of people's power. In 1989 these were given additional powers in a context of administrative decentralization and were re-named Nuevos Consejos Populares or New People's Councils.

CUC or chavito – peso Cubano convertible – Cuban convertible peso

cuentapropistas – Cubans who work on their own account or who are self-employed. This category of workers was eliminated in the Revolutionary Offensive of 1968, which did away with the market and private enterprise. In 2008 when Raúl Castro took over the helm of state, one of the economic reforms he brought about restored the private small business sector and established a broad range of self-employment possibilities. In 2013 the government announced that up to 500,000 state workers would be let go and that they would be expected to create their own jobs and source of livelihood.

DNM – Dirección Nacional de las Militias – National Directorate of Militias

EAC – Escuela al Campo – School in the Countryside. These schools were set up all over Cuba after the revolution and transformed Cuban the rural population and workers into literate and educated citizens in a short period.

ECLAC – La Comisión Económica para América Latina y el Caribe – United Nations Economic Commission for Latin America and the Caribbean

FAO – Food and Agriculture Organization of the United Nations

FAR – Fuerzas Armadas Revolucionarias – Revolutionary Armed Forces of Cuba

FMC – Federación de Mujeres Cubanas – Federation of Cuban Women

Gini Index – an international standard index widely used by economists to measure income inequality on a scale from 1 to 10, although results do not reflect standards of healthcare and education.

Great Debate – a period in Cuban economic history in 1963 and 1964 during which two radically different models of economic development were debated. Che Guevara emphasized the importance of moral incentives in promoting economic development, while the proponents of more orthodox economics argued the need for material incentives in the belief that without such incentives people would not strive to achieve and that the economy would suffer. See Guevara, 2006.

HDI – Human Development Index (of the United Nations Development Programme). This is a composite statistic of life expectancy, education and income indices used by the UNDP to rank countries into four tiers of human development. It was created by the Pakistani and Indian economists Mahbub ul Haq and Amartya Sen in 1990. Results are published yearly by the UNDP in their HD report (see below).

HDR – *Human Development Report* (of the United Nations Development Programme). These have been issued annually by the UNDP since 1990 and report on conditions of human development (as conceived by the UNDP) worldwide.

hombre nuevo – new man, or new person – a term coined by Che Guevara to refer to a process of revolutionary transformation in individuals' awareness and concern for others, for community and for society as a whole, which concern comes to supersede preoccupation solely with one's individual interests. This new person is formed by his or her involvement in socialist revolution and becomes the ideal citizen who is imbued with a socialist consciousness.

hombre novísimo – This term was coined during the Special Period (see below), which was marked by a new notion of an ideal citizen. The term means, literally, an even newer socialist person.

human development – a concept elaborated by the UNDP in its annual HDR (*Human Development Report*). Defined theoretically as the expansion of choice for individuals in society, it was designed to capture the social dimensions of development: the opportunity to earn or access income to sustain human welfare, education or schooling, health and life expectancy.

imperialism – the exercise by a state of its power to advance its ostensible national interests which are in fact identified with the those of the capitalist class and their international corporate operations

indicative planning – When using indicative planning, a state influences, subsidizes, provides grants, and taxes to affect the economy. Indicative planning differs from *directive* or *mandatory planning*, in which quotas and mandatory output requirements are imposed.

INRA – Instituto Nacional de Reforma Agraria – National Institute for Agrarian Reform

JUCEPLAN – Junta Central de Planificación – Central Planning Board. This board of economic planning was instituted after the Revolution; Che Guevara was appointed its "technical secretary" in 1962.

latifundia – a term originating in ancient Rome and later used by Spanish colonial regimes in reference to large landholdings, particularly those given by land-grant to military officers and other beneficiaries deemed worthy. *Latifundia* were generally used to grow crops for export. Contrasted with *minifundios* or very small landholdings.

libreta – The *libreta de abastecimiento,* or Cuban ration book, was introduced in 1963 as a means of rationing food and ensuring access to minimum supplies for all Cubans. Despite rumours of the system ending, it still exists.

means of production – The physical, non-human inputs used in production including both the instruments of labour such as tools, factories and infrastructure, and subjects of labour: natural resources and raw materials. Ownership of the means of production and control over the surplus product generated by their operation is the fundamental factor in delineating different economic systems. Capitalism is defined by private ownership and control over the means of production, where the surplus product becomes a source of unearned income for business interests. By contrast, socialism is defined as public ownership of the means of production so that surplus product accrues to society at large.

MEDICC – Medical Education Cooperation with Cuba. This is a U.S.-based non-profit organization working to enhance cooperation among U.S., Cuban and global health-care communities. Its aims are equitable access and quality care, and it allows the Cuban experience of socialist healthcare to inform global debate, practice, policies and cooperation in healthcare.

New World Group – inspired by Lloyd Best in 1957, a loosely organized group of intellectuals, educators, cultural workers, writers and activists mainly from the Anglophone Caribbean or who have Caribbean origins and interests

OLPP – Órganos Locales del Poder Popular – Local Bodies of People's Power

ONE – Oficina Nacional de Estadísticas – National Office of Statistics of Cuba

PCC – Partido Comunista de Cuba – Communist Party of Cuba

peasant – a smallholding family farmer immersed in the conditions and precapitalist relations of developing societies (see also *campesinos*)

proletarianization – See endnote 2, Introduction.

proletariat – the working class; those who, dispossessed of their means of production, are compelled to exchange their labour for a living wage

RP – Programa de Rectificación – Rectification Program – a program of economic policies introduced between 1988 and 1990 by the Cuban leadership to counteract the slowdown of economic growth and sluggishness of economic activity

social property – property in the means of production that is held in common or collectivized; as opposed to private property.

Special Period – El Período Especial – the Cuban leadership's term to describe the economic crisis (including the fall by as much as 35 percent in national output, or the GDP) in the early 1990s, following the collapse of the Soviet Union

UBPC – Unidad Básica de Producción Cooperativa – Basic Unit of Cooperative Production. A form of agricultural cooperative which replaced many Cuban state farms in 1993. The UBPC system linked workers more closely to the land by giving them indefinite usufruct over it; it established incentives by tying workers' earnings to overall unit production and increased workers' managerial autonomy.

UNDP – United Nations Development Programme

UNEAC – Unión de Escritores y Artistas de Cuba – Union of Writers and Artists of Cuba

UNESCO – United Nations Educational, Scientific and Cultural Organization

UNRISD – United Nations Research Institute for Social Development

WHO – World Health Organisation (an agency of the United Nations)

Introduction

Cuba, the main still-vibrant socialist experiment in the history of the Western world, is enmeshed in a process of imminent transformation. For the Revolution to survive the forces assailing it from within and without, it will need to tack well to the fierce winds of change blowing over the world capitalist system. It has done so before, although not without making mistakes (and attempts to rectify them). In fact, an as-yet not entirely explained mystery is how the Cuban Revolution managed to survive the crisis and perfect storm associated with the collapse of socialism in the early 1990s. But the Revolution did survive it, prompting some to argue that if Cuba survived that crisis it could survive virtually anything thrown at it.

But the leadership and current administration did not and does not take this view. It is all too aware of what is at stake and that it cannot call on Cubans endlessly to tighten their belts and absorb the high social costs of adjusting to change and the dictates of government policy. Another round of reforms to the Revolution, what Cubans call "updating the model," is clearly called for and is now underway. The leadership and the entire country, in the current climate of world development, is engaged in seeking how best to make this adjustment and change direction. Raúl Castro, at the helm of the ship of state has declared, "either we correct our mistakes or we sink." At stake in this crisis — in addition to preserving the Revolution's achievements in human development — is not only Cuba's capacity to chart its own path of national development, but socialism itself. The question is whether Cuba will be forced to cut a capitalist road towards national development as Russia, China and Vietnam have done in recent years, or whether it can continue to lead the forces of socialist transformation in the twenty-first century.

This book addresses this question by reviewing features of Cuban socialism that have helped the country survive one crisis after another as well as more than fifty years of hostile actions by one of the world's most aggressive imperialist superpowers perched perilously close to Cuba's shores. This book's central thesis is that the Cuban Revolution has survived a great array of assaults over the years, and will quite possibly survive the current crisis as well because of certain features of the socialist project of human development, one that sets Cuba apart from other socialist endeavours. To some extent, Cuba's socialist course can be likened to the work of economists of the United Nations Development Programme (UNDP), which in the 1990s launched the idea of human development as an alternative to the neoliberal model of capitalist development, as a way of saving capitalism from its internal contradictions and self-destructive tendencies: of saving capitalism from itself. The difference between human development as conceived by the UNDP and "socialist human development," in the case of the project motivating and underlying the Cuban Revolution, is that the former is predicated on capitalism as the operating system. This book takes the view that capitalism by its very nature is antithetical to the creation of a truly human society, and that Cuban socialism, in spite of its structural problems and other deficiencies, can still be a beacon lighting a course to a better world.

The argument of the book

Chapter One reconstructs the itinerary of the human development idea and the advance of two related yet fundamentally different projects to create a society modelled on this idea. The United States and its allies at the end of World War II were concerned that countries seeking to liberate themselves from the yoke of European colonialism might turn to socialism rather than to capitalism in their strategies for national development. This led to the project of international cooperation for development, and "international development," as a field of study, was born. The Bretton Woods framework had been in place since 1944, with its rules and institutions for governing international economic relations within world capitalism. Within this system, development had been understood and advanced for some three decades as a matter of "economic growth," or the expansion of society's forces of production. The 1980s, however, saw a sharp turn toward free market capitalism that led to a search for a new paradigm. This sharp turn was motivated by a "new world order" designed to liberate the "forces of economic freedom" from the regulatory constraints of the welfare-development state. It led t o a new way of understanding development in terms of the freedom and enhanced capacity of individuals in society to realize their full human potential; this new concern for individual development became known as *human development*. The aim of this approach to development was to reform the system in order to save capitalism from its propensity to crisis and to humanize it. This chapter tells the story of this inquiry and it tells another as-yet untold story about an entirely different approach to human development: the story of the Cuban Revolution.

Chapter Two briefly traces the origins of the Cuban Revolution, highlighting the human development project and the choice socialism made to meet that project's system requirements. Subsequent chapters outline the major dimensions of this project. Chapter Three focuses on the dynamics of "revolutionary consciousness," identifying it as a fundamental ethos of socialism as understood by the Cuban revolutionaries. Here it is argued that socialism, understood as a project of creating a new type of society in which everyone is able to realize their human potential, requires a cultural revolution. It requires a break from the culture of possessive individualism and of grasping materialism in which individuals make calculations of self-interest in choosing their different courses of action and interaction with other members of society. What socialism required, according to Che Guevara, a chief ideologue of the Cuban Revolution, was a new ethic: a social and cultural transformation which called upon men and women, imbued with a new revolutionary socialist consciousness, to act as social beings bound together by bonds of mutual support. These new men and new women would also be bound as part of a broader collective: an egalitarian society in which, "the free development of each is a condition for the free development of all." In this context the Revolution was conceived as a process of constant struggle in "the progressive formation of new values" (Castro, 1992).

> Ernesto Guevara, commonly known as "Che" was an Argentine Marxist revolutionary, physician, author, guerrilla leader and social and political theorist. As a young medical student, he travelled through South America by motorcycle and was radicalized by the poverty, hunger and disease that he witnessed. His desire to help overturn what he viewed as capitalist exploitation and imperialist subjugation by the U.S. prompted his participation in Guatemala's social reforms under president Arbenz, whose eventual CIA-assisted overthrow at the behest of the United Fruit Company solidified his political ideology. Later, in Mexico City, Guevara met Raúl and Fidel Castro, joined their twenty-sixth-of-July Movement, and sailed to Cuba aboard the yacht Granma with the intention of overthrowing U.S.-backed Cuban dictator Batista. Following the successful 1959 insurgency Guevara took on a number of key roles in the new government, including the institution of land reform as minister of industries and helping spearhead a successful nationwide literacy campaign. Additionally he was a prolific writer and diarist. His experiences and study of Marxism-Leninism led him to posit that third world underdevelopment was the intrinsic result of imperialism, neocolonialism and monopoly capitalism, and that the only remedy was revolution. As a result of his poetic invocations for class struggle and concern to create a revolutionary consciousness of "new men and new women" driven by moral rather than material incentives, he is upheld as an icon by diverse movements for revolutionary change.

Chapter Four turns to the notion of social solidarity as a fundamental pillar of Cuban socialism. The French revolutionaries in 1789 rallied to the cause of social revolution under the banner of "liberty, equality and fraternity,"[1] or solidarity. However, in subsequent political developments and revolutionary processes of the nineteenth and twentieth centuries, the focus was on freedom (in liberal discourse) or equality (in socialist discourse). The idea of social solidarity withered on the vine of capitalist and socialist development until it was resuscitated by the Cuban revolutionaries as a fundamental aim and value. When they turned their attention to solidarity and endeavoured to bring it about, the meaning of the associated ideas of freedom and equality was more completely realized. This chapter looks at the policy and political dynamics of the idea of social and international solidarity in the context of the Cuban Revolution.

In Chapter Five, the book turns towards a fundamental principle of socialism in all its forms and towards another dimension of socialist human development in the Cuban context. Equality is a fundamental issue for human development under capitalism as well, but there it is transmuted into the principle of equity, that is, not as a matter of an equality of condition, but as an equality of opportunity for individuals to advance themselves or realize their own capabilities (UNDP, 2010). It is recognized that capitalist societies are class-divided with structured inequalities in social conditions that vary by class. Also, it is assumed that the human development of these societies is possible as long as individuals are free to act and take advantage of their opportunities. In theory, governments ensure a relatively even playing field: they provide an equality of opportunity for individuals to realize their human potential according to their abilities. Under socialism, however, the issue is not equality as a formal right or opportunity available to each individual as an individual, but equality in a socialist context is a substantive condition that is widely shared or given to all members of society. Human development under socialism is therefore measured by the degree to which equality of social conditions is achieved.

Chapter Six turns towards the idea of freedom and the politics of socialist human development inside the Cuban Revolution. This question of development as freedom is crucial and very controversial in the Cuban context. Bourgeois liberals and other critics have long argued the existence of a democratic deficit or the lack of freedom in Cuba. The chapter begins with a brief discussion of the different meanings attached to the idea of freedom, including what it means in the context of the Cuban Revolution. While the ideologues and theorists of human development at the UNDP understand freedom in social liberal terms as an expansion of choice and opportunities available to individuals for them to realize their human potential, for the Cuban revolutionaries freedom is social or collective, not personal. Following Marx in his socialist humanist (rather than historical materialist) conception, freedom is understood as freedom from want and exploitation, emancipation from relations and conditions of class rule and imperialist exploitation.

Chapter Seven is concerned with the development dynamics of agriculture and the transformation of a society and economy based on agriculture, into an urban society based on modern industry. When conceptualized in terms of the long-term and large-scale transformation of agrarian societies (which were based on precapitalist relationships of production into a modern industrial society) the agrarian question had to do with different national paths towards industrial capitalism. However, this question can also be raised in the context of socialist development and the path taken by some countries towards socialism. What about the socialist development of agriculture? The celebrated cases of Russia and

China are telling and disturbing, pointing as they do to a rather inhuman process of forced collectivization that engaged forces of systemic and political violence. These paralleled the harsh and brutal consequences of the capitalist development process. Indeed, some argue that in the case of Russia and China the transition towards socialism was even more violent and bloody, involving as it did not only the dispossession of small-scale agricultural producers and "peasant" farmers,[2] and their forced abandonment of agriculture, their livelihoods and rural communities, but mass starvation that by some accounts encompassed tens of millions of peasant farmers.

What form did the agrarian transformation take in Cuba from an agriculture-based system into a modern urban-centred one? And under what conditions has socialist agriculture in Cuba evolved? This is the central focus of Chapter Seven. The chapter argues that certain unique developments in the history of the Revolution led it to diverge in crucial ways: in its socialist development of agriculture and from the agrarian and agricultural experiences of other nations that attempted socialist revolution in the twentieth century. In fact, it could be argued that, notwithstanding the persistence of conditions that recall the Soviet model of centralized planning, the form taken by socialist agriculture in Cuba is better suited to achieving the goals of human development and ecological sustainability than conventional models, either capitalist or socialist.

Chapter Eight briefly analyzes the meaning of economic reforms implemented during Raúl Castro's presidency since 2008 and ongoing attempts to update the model of Cuban socialism. The first part of the chapter reviews structural problems that have beset the Revolution almost from the beginning. These problems can be traced back to the need to adjust the economy to the workings of global capitalism and to a fateful "Revolutionary Offensive" against capitalism in 1968. This process of adjustment clearly was not free from errors, some of them very serious indeed. For example, as part of the regime's Revolutionary Offensive, all forms of private enterprise and the market economy as a whole was jettisoned, abolishing not only capitalism but the remaining vestiges of a market economy and small businesses in the private sector.

In retrospect, another major mistake — although the Revolutionary regime had few if any options, given the hostile actions of the U.S. regime — was the decision to align the economy to that of the Soviet Union. This was driven by Cuba's desperate need for oil and technology, which were exchanged for sugar, the production conditions for which were ideal in Cuba. This strategy led the country not only into a path of dependent development, dependence on the Soviet Union, but more importantly, dependence on the production of a single export crop. The long-term consequences of this strategy are strikingly evident today in loss of food security and sovereignty, which required Cuba to import from a third to a half of its food products on the world market, much of it from the United States.[3]

The third section of the chapter reviews the contradictions and continuities associated with this adjustment process, and the fourth part discusses the far-reaching reforms announced by the administration in 2008 with Raúl Castro's assuming the helm of state. These reforms were instituted in the wake of the deliberations on the economy and reform by the Sixth Congress of the Cuban Communist Party (PCC). The chapter ends with a series of reflections on the scope, meaning and likely outcomes of recent efforts to update the model. At issue here is whether Cuba will follow the Soviet Union, China and Vietnam down the road of capitalist development or whether Cuban socialism will survive its latest challenge.

The Cuban Revolution in an era of neoliberal globalization

By 1975 socialism was more or less institutionalized in the basic form taken by Cuba today. This is to say, it was based on the principles of socialist humanism and the search for "complete equality and freedom" (Fidel Castro) and "full democracy" (Harnecker).[4] But a decade later the economic engine of the Revolution, fuelled by a combination of moral exhortations and material incentives, had begun to run out of steam. And in 1990, after several years of experimentation with policy measures designed to rectify the situation, Cuba entered (rather, it was pushed by external forces) what has been called el Período Especial, or the Special Period, the conditions of which threatened to scuttle the revolutionary process and the very survival of the system.

Behind these conditions was the collapse of socialism in the U.S.S.R. and Eastern Europe, creating conditions of a major economic downturn and production crisis that threatened the very survival of the Revolution and Cuban socialism. In response to this crisis, the regime was compelled to introduce economic reforms, which, by many accounts, themselves threatened to undermine the socialist human development project of the Revolution. Yet the Revolution not only survived the crisis but over the next decade and a half it took a slow but steady road to economic recovery, maintaining its social welfare and human development programs intact in the process. No schools or clinics were closed. The government managed to maintain the superstructure of human development as well the operational social programs that delivered essential services. Not only did Cuba improve its standing on the UNDP's Human Development Index (HDI) — from eighty-first in 1992 to fifty-first in 2010 — but it somehow managed to maintain overwhelming support for the Revolution under the most adverse conditions and forced austerity.

Most surprising in this context has been the Revolution's commitment to international solidarity in the form of medical and education assistance. With the small population base of eleven million and an island economy with low levels of economic growth and per-capita incomes, Cuba has managed to deliver a program of international solidarity that puts to shame the community of countries and organizations engaged in international cooperation for human development. Over 25 percent of Cuba's medical professionals, teachers and technicians have served in other countries. Thousands of young people from all over the globe go to Cuba to study in the highly recognized schools and universities. Chapter Four looks at these figures in more detail. Some analysts (James Petras, for example) have cautioned that this unprecedented level of support to human development in the developing world, and Cuba's continuing commitment to international solidarity, might have had too high a cost to domestic solidarity and to the Revolution. Nevertheless, all indications are that the program has the support of most Cubans, and this raises questions about how Cuba has managed to retain this support under the most adverse of conditions.

The answer to this question lies in certain features of the Cuban model. First, there is the commitment to building *la conciencia* — revolutionary conscious-ness — as a strategy of socialist development, and to do so by means of the active engagement of Cubans in the revolutionary process. This achievement (the ability to retain this support for the Revolution) can be attributed to the participatory and democratic form of Cuban socialism, which runs counter to the image that most non-Cubans, including scholars, have of Cuba. Indeed it is commonplace among non-Cuban scholars to stress Cuba's democratic deficit: "Castroism" (command politics centred on the person of Fidel); the verticalism and vanguardism that purportedly characterize Cuba's single-party-dominated political system (Harris, 1992); its authoritarianism (Horowitz, 1977); bureaucratic centralism (Huberman & Sweezy, 1960); and more generally and significantly, the intolerance of dissent. All these critics tar with the same brush and lump together legitimate dissent, constructive critics and subversives in the service of Washington.

Notwithstanding this criticism, a close look at the Revolution from the inside suggests a different picture. This other picture is one of social democracy and active participation of ordinary Cubans not only in the affairs of state and public policy-making, but in local development which improves conditions that affect Cubans in their communities, their workplaces and everyday lives (Rosendahl, 1997; Taylor, 2009; Uriarte, 2008). The institutional framework for this democratic governance and participatory development is provided by the Órganos Locales del Poder Popular (Local Bodies of People's Power; OLPP), which were first established in 1976 but which were later modified in 1992 with the institution of a new system of Consejos Populares (People's Councils). Within the framework of these institutions, Cubans are able to participate actively in policy-making, not just in the form of mass mobilizations, but also in decision-making regarding both national and local development (García Brigos, 2001; Roman, 2003; Uriarte, 2008).

In the 1990s a critical feature of public action (government intervention with popular participation) included hundreds of workers' parliaments in which ordinary Cubans in their workplaces and communities were actively engaged in the process of presenting, debating and discussing appropriate measures to be taken (Roman, 2003). It is evident that engagement in the ongoing revolutionary process was a critical factor in sustaining a revolutionary consciousness and a socialist ethos, and in sustaining continued support for the Revolution. A feature of the response to the crisis and globalization of the 1990s was a turn to local development and the institution of actions taken at the initiative of people at the municipal level.

In other parts of Latin America there has been a similar turn towards local development, within the framework of a new development paradigm and a post-Washington Consensus[5] on the need for a more socially inclusive form of development based on a policy of decentralization (Dilla Alfonso & Núñez, 1997; Rondinelli, McCullough & Johnson, 1989; Rao, 2002; Veltmeyer, 2007). In Cuba, however, there was no need for this policy. The Local Bodies of People's Power (OLPP) provided the institutional support and the space for a participatory form of politics and development, allowing Cubans to engage directly in decision-making regarding both national policy and in relation to conditions that affect them in their everyday lives. They also point to local development as a strategic response to the dynamics of globalization and to the municipality as the locus of this development (Guzón, 2003; Vazquez, 2007). Chapter Six examines this reality of Cuban participation and looks at some other examples of popular participation in the context of Latin American socialist development.

1. Socialism and
Human Development

Since the collapse of the Soviet Union and the Eastern Bloc and the strengthening of the United States' economic blockade (characterized in the Washington Consensus), many "experts," especially from within the ramparts of the American Empire, have predicted the imminent or inevitable collapse of the Cuban Revolution. However, not only has the socialist regime managed to survive one challenge after another — and the 1990s saw the most serious to date — but it managed successfully to soldier through changes that toppled one socialist regime after another, and that brought many capitalist regimes to the brink of financial disaster in the (dis)order of neoliberal globalization. Not only has the Cuban Revolution survived but its notable and widely acknowledged achievements at the level of human development continue to baffle analysts and Cuba-watchers worldwide. On this issue, the begrudging comments of James Wolfensohn, President of the World Bank, are telling: he acknowledged that "Cuba has done a great job on education and health" and said, "it does not embarrass me to admit it." He added, "[Cubans] should be congratulated on what they've done" (quoted in Lobe, 2001).

Yet, as Saney notes (2003) in his brilliant albeit brief reconstruction of the Cuban Revolution, in spite of substantive achievements at the level of human development, "the island continues to be ignored by both development theorists and the technocrats in charge of implementing and administering programs that are designed to lead to the improved well-being of the world's people." He notes that a 1997 World Bank Discussion Paper, "Poverty Reduction and Human Development in the Caribbean," did not contain a single mention of Cuba. Patricia Gray, in *Latin America: Its Future in the Global Economy*, also does not give Cuba a solitary comment. In a *New Internationalist* issue on "The Liberation of Latin America," in May 2003, which focused on the region's challenges to neoliberalism, Cuba is not discussed at all. And Osvaldo de Rivero in *The Myth of Development* (2001:183) dismisses Cuba as marginal in today's world.

This book argues, on the contrary, that the Cuban Revolution has much to teach the world, and that it warrants a closer look as a model of socialist human development. A re-reading of the Cuban Revolution from this angle allows us to confront several unresolved issues in the theory of socialist humanism and in the

9

notion of "human development" popularized by the UNDP as a way of saving capitalism from its internal contradictions.[1] The UNDP notion of human development is predicated on capitalism, even though this is never acknowledged. The concern of the economists at the UNDP and of those at other agencies of international cooperation for development, is to give a human face to a capitalist development process that is anything but human. All this is done in an effort to determine the best policy mix and institutional reforms needed to sustain the capitalist process.

The chapter that follows argues that precise forms and particular conditions of socialist human development explain the survival of Cuban socialism and call for a closer look at the history of the Revolution. Two features of this model, it is argued, 1. the construction of a socialist ethic (revolutionary consciousness) and 2. popular participation in public policy formulation (people power), were critical factors in Cuba's successful navigation through global capitalist development and the survival of the Revolution in the face of unprecedented economic and political challenges.

Not only does the recent trajectory of the Cuban Revolution challenge the conventional wisdom of bourgeois social science and the UNDP's approach to human development, but it also highlights the debate surrounding the conditions and instrumentalities needed to achieve human development. We see capitalism and socialism more clearly contrasted; we see the contraposition of a strong and interventionist state against the forces of the free market, privatization and neoliberalism. Our glimpse into the conceptual and ethical foundations of the Cuban Revolution also throws light on certain problems of socialist development and how best to proceed in rebuilding socialism in the twenty-first century.

Human development: The itinerary of an idea

The contemporary concept of human development[2] can be traced back to the rallying cry for revolutionary change in the French Revolution. This cry took the form of three ideas advanced in the belief in the power of human reason to bring about a different society more in accord with human nature. The ideas were those of freedom, equality and fraternity, or solidarity.

Over the course of the nineteenth and twentieth centuries, these three ideas were acted upon as points of reference in diverse struggles to advance the human development project and to resolve what Marx had seen as a fundamental conflict between society as it was and as it ought to be. In the long process of social change and development, these ideas were transmuted into several ideologies that served to mobilize change in the direction of freedom or equality, and they were institutionalized in varying forms of practice associated with capitalist and socialist development. Without falling into the idealist trap of imagining this process as simply the march of "the Idea" in the process of its self-development, it is nevertheless possible to identify a number of key moments in what could be described as the dialectic of an idea[3]: that of human development.

The process of this dialectic can be reconstructed in terms of the following moments:

- a call for change in revolutionary France, acting on ideas (freedom, equality, solidarity) constructed by the *philosophes* of the eighteenth century Enlightenment in response to the social conditions of oligarchic class rule and the tyranny of church and state;

- the battle for democracy: a political movement to overthrow authoritarian class rule and the institution of the monarchy and to replace it with a democratic state in which the people (the *demos*) are free to participate and to formulate laws that represent the general will. In a political system that embodied this ideal the freedom of individuals would be given to all citizens, and that freedom would be restricted only by the requirements of security and those of trespass on the freedom of others;

- a socialist movement that is governed by a belief in the need for revolutionary change, a fundamental overhaul of the economic and social system in the direction of equality. In Marx's formulation of socialist humanism, freedom is understood as emancipation from relations of exploitation and oppression. Solidarity, in a utopian socialist formulation, is seen as that of people as social beings bound together by bonds of mutual support;

- the idea of progress transmuted into a belief in the human need for freedom from want and for freedom to improve one's economic situation and social conditions on the basis of economic growth or the expansion of the forces of economic production. This theory of economic growth was formulated by Adam Smith on the premise that its system requirements are provided by capitalism: a system of commodity production in which goods are produced for sale on the market; in which the value of commodities (the form taken by social production) is determined by the embodiment of labour-power; and in which the factors of production (land, capital, labour) are freed from social or political constraint;

- a socialist revolution, the conditions for which were actualized in Russia in the early twentieth century. In conditions that prevailed at the time, the project of socialist transformation was advanced through the agency of the state, with a fundamental concern not so much for individual freedom (the fundamental concern of bourgeois liberalism) as for equality: for socializing production as means of abolishing class divisions and creating conditions that are equal for all;

- construction of a capitalist welfare state in the context of a major involution in the system of capitalist production, the Great Depression, that threatened the very survival of capitalism. The foundations of capitalist welfare were laid in the 1930s with the incorporation of a number of socialist principles. It would take another three decades for it to assume its contemporary form as the welfare state;

- transmutation of the idea of progress into the project of economic development advanced by 1. a process of productive and social transformation (capitalist development of the forces of production) and by 2. international cooperation with nation-building efforts of economically backward areas of the world that are struggling to escape the yoke and ties of colonialism. Subsequently, this idea of economic progress was combined with the ideals of freedom and equality and this gave development a social dimension, becoming the project of human development; and
- the Cuban Revolution as an embodiment of the fundamental ideals and organizing principles of socialist humanism: freedom as emancipation, equality as a social condition for all, and solidarity as unity in struggle.

Dynamics of capitalist and socialist development

The dynamics of capitalism in its development of the forces of production (capitalist development) have been presented as a process of productive and social transformation in the transition of a traditional, pre-capitalist and agrarian form of society towards a modern industrial capitalist system. The theoretical representation of this process has been constructed in three ways: 1. industrialization, the transformation of agrarian societies and economies into industrial ones; 2. capitalist development, the transformation of societies of small-scale direct producers into a wage-earning proletariat; and 3. modernization, the transformation of a traditional culture into a modern one.

The capitalist development process, in terms of changes in society's modes of production, has been conceptualized in many ways. A brief outline follows (Desai, 2000).

- The period from 1500 to 1800, dominated by mercantile capitalism, which laid the foundations of the capitalist system by means of a process of primitive accumulation in which the direct producers are separated from the means of production.
- The period from 1800 to 1870, of industrial capitalism, characterized by the generalization of capital-labour or wage relationship, the development of the factory system and a competitive struggle of small capital in an expanding capitalist market.
- The period from 1870 to 1914, dominated by European imperialism, which laid the foundations of monopoly capitalism or, as Lenin saw it, imperialism. The period was characterized by the concentration and centralization of capital, the merger of industrial and financial capital, the export of capital and the formation of monopoly capitalism. Multinational corporations dominated the markets in which they operated. A territorial division of the world economy was effected with a process of colonization.
- The period from 1917 to 1944, characterized by a process of capitalist and

socialist industrialization and a deep crisis in capitalist production. The construction of a capitalist welfare state began, two world wars set the world in turmoil, and the British Empire collapsed.

- The period from 1945 to 1970 of rapid system-wide economic growth: the Golden Age of Capitalism, based on an accord between labour and capital in which the former would participate in the productivity gains of economic growth and in conditions of a liberal capitalist world order (the Bretton Woods system). This period also saw the emergence of an ideological conflict between capitalism and socialism, a decolonization process featuring sociopolitical movements of national liberation and the evolution of a development state.

- The period from 1973 to 1982 of transition characterized by a system-wide crisis in capitalist production, a multi-faceted restructuring of the system, the launch of a global class war between capital and labour, and the construction of a development state in the global south.

- The period from 1983 to the present has been dominated by the mobility of global capital in the era of neoliberal globalization (free market capitalism) — or what David Harvey has called the "short history of neoliberalism" — and by the construction of a new world order in which the forces of economic freedom are liberated from the constraints of the welfare development state.

From Bretton Woods to a new world order of neoliberal globalization

The contemporary phase of capitalist development can be traced back to the construction of the Bretton Woods system in 1944, at an international conference held in Bretton Woods, Maryland, by the victorious capitalist powers. This system provided both a set of rules for governing international economic relations among nations (global governance) and an institutional framework for the form that capitalism would take, namely state-led development. Within the framework of the Bretton Woods world order, the idea of development was advanced as a way of ensuring that governments in countries of the so-called economically "backward" parts of the disintegrating British empire would not fall prey to the lure of communism and take a socialist path paved by the U.S.S.R. towards national development.

Another front in the project of establishing development with international cooperation was opened up in the 1960s in the wake of the Cuban Revolution. Efforts were made to appease the fires of revolutionary ferment brewing in various parts of the emerging American Empire and to prevent the formation of another Cuba. This front took the form of "integrated rural development." It involved the active intervention of the state in the redistribution of market-generated incomes in the interest of equity (growth with equity). Development in this form was designed as a means of turning the rural poor (large numbers of landless or near-landless "proletarianized" farmers) away from the revolutionary social movements they were mounting (often joined by organized labour in the cities).

This project was the velvet glove on the hard fist of state repression and imperial power. In the 1970s this local front of the war on the rural poor (represented as a war against rural poverty) coincided with yet another front in this war launched by the World Bank on behalf of the organizations engaged in the project of international cooperation, in the form of the "basic needs" approach to international development.

The agency for implementing this strategy was the development state or what we might well call the welfare development state. The aim of the strategy, not to put too fine a point on it, was to offset mounting pressures for revolutionary change by instituting state-led reforms into the operating capitalist system, regulating capital in its global operations while also providing for both welfare and development.

From the Washington Consensus to a Post-Washington Consensus
The irony is that these efforts at reform were instituted under conditions of a system-wide production crisis, which reduced fiscal resources and pushed many states into economic crises. The conditions of these crises, combined with a conservative counterrevolution in development thinking and practice, led to the call for a new world order in which the forces of economic freedom were released from the regulatory constraints of the development state. In 1983 a region-wide debt crisis provided the leverage on the governments to respond to this call in the form of a program of structural reform mandated as the process of admission into the new world order. However, by the end of the decade it was increasingly evident that the new model of neoliberal globalization was economically dysfunctional and politically unsustainable. The exceedingly high social costs of structural adjustment were generating widespread forces of resistance that threatened to undermine the stability of neoliberal regimes.

In the late 1980s, barely five years into the new world order of neoliberal globalization, the recognition that capitalist states had gone too far in the direction of the free market (Rodrik, Stiglitz) led to the formation of a new post-Washington Consensus. This new consensus focused on the need to secure a "better balance between state and market" and to create conditions of a more socially inclusive and more equitable and participatory form of development that would empower the poor (Craig & Porter, 2006; Ocampo, 2005; Sandbrook, Edelman, Heller & Teichman, 2007).

The agency for this development was a partnership between the state and civil society, with international cooperation and social participation. The model that could serve this policy agenda was provided by the UNDP in the form of "sustainable human development." It prescribed policies that combined administrative decentralization with a new social policy, investment in health and in education (human capital formation): a new development paradigm.

Socialist humanism and the Cuban Revolution
In Russia the socialization of production and the transformation of the "peasantry" into a proletariat took force and violence. As a process it was not in the least participatory. At the time, up to 80 percent of the population was made up of poor farmers, hardly the social basis of Marx's envisioned socialism. Hence the state instituted a process of socialist development of the forces of production on the basis of a model (industrialization, modernization and proletarianization) that did not differ substantially from the capitalist development model, except for the heavy hand of the state in the process of productive and social transformation.

In Cuba the approach to socialist development was quite different. For one thing, there was no forced socialization and collectivization. The population was actively engaged in the process of decision-making and public policy. The difference is not incidental. In fact, it could be argued that the Cuban Revolution was based on a significantly different model: established on a very different foundation and designed as a project of socialist humanism.

The conceptual and ethical foundation of socialism in this form, it can be argued, rests on the following five pillars:

1. a revolutionary consciousness and socialist ethos forged under conditions of a cultural revolution;
2. a fundamental commitment to universal human rights and the social welfare of all;
3. a system-defining concern for equality that would create an egalitarian society in which "the free development of each," as Marx argued, "is a condition for the free development of all";
4. the idea of freedom, understood not in a liberal sense but in a conception that can be traced back to Marx in his early works and beyond Marx back to the eighteenth-century Enlightenment idea of progress; and
5. social solidarity, a fundamental value for the utopian socialists of the nineteenth century, the labour movement of the twentieth century and the communalism of several indigenous social movements in Latin America.

Dimensions of socialist human development

Human development, as presented in the UNDP's Human Development Reports (HDR), is conceived in social liberal terms as "the enlargement of choice and opportunities for individuals to advance themselves" (Haq, 2000; A. Sen, 1989). In these terms ("development as freedom"), the social condition of human development is measured as an amalgam of three variables: life expectancy, school enrolment and literacy, and per-capita income.

With human development conceptualized and measured in this way, Cuba was placed by the UNDP in the category of a country with a low level of per-capita income, which is the measure of economic growth as the World Bank understands it. But the UNDP categorized Cuba as having a "high level of human development." Of course, this difference in interpretation reflects the weight of the variables used to measure levels of social development.

When the UNDP began to publish the HDR in 1990, Cuba had just experienced five years of decidedly slow growth and a "rectification" campaign designed to redress this slowdown, and the country was just about to enter the Special Period in its revolutionary process. Under conditions of a major economic downturn, with a fall of 35 percent in national output, Cuba was ranked at a "medium level of human development" (sixty-second out of 130 countries) on the UNDP's Human Development Index (HDI).

By 1992, in the throes of the Special Period crisis, Cuba's ranking dropped to eighty-first, reflecting the income factor in the Index. In 1994 its ranking slipped another eight points. The positive impact of the economic reforms that the government was compelled to introduce in adjusting to the forces of globalization was reflected in the rather dramatic improvement in Cuba's ranking on the HDI in 1999 (fifty-eighth). However, a study on the state of human development commissioned by the UNDP in 1996 and then in 1999 made it clear that the most significant feature of Cuba's record of human development in the 1990s was not the parabola of economic growth it had been through but its ability to maintain the infrastructure of social development.

Throughout the crisis, though the nutritional coverage and caloric value of the *libreta* (ration card) was reduced (for an estimated 20 percent of families), well below a level that would meet basic needs for food, not a school was closed, nor a clinic. The results were rather surprising. Notwithstanding the near collapse of the economy and the system-challenging economic reforms, and in spite of the financial resource pressures on its system-defining social programs, Cuba's ranking on key human development indicators improved in the latter half of the Special Period. The country ranked fifty-eighth on the HDI in 1999, and fifty-sixth in 2000. Its human development performance in the twenty-first century has been such (fifty-first of 177 in 2009) that it placed in the "high human development" category. As noted earlier, this provoked the president of the World Bank to say that Cuba was doing something right (Lobe, 2001).

2. The Revolution as
Socialist Human Development

The notion of human development advanced by the UNDP, which is used to rank countries in its annual flagship publication *Human Development Report* (HDR), is predicated on capitalism as the operating system, even though no mention is ever made of this. The reason for this omission is that capitalism supposes itself to be uniquely configured around the idea of freedom, which is to say the freedom of individuals to pursue opportunities and advance their own interests in the pursuit of life-enhancing goals, or what has been called "human flourishing" (Deneulin & Shahani, 2009). However, given the propensity of capitalism towards class division and uneven development, the concern of economists at the UNDP and other agencies of international cooperation for development has been to give a human face to a capitalist development process that is anything but humane, and to do this so as to determine the best policy mix and institutional reforms needed to sustain the development process.

Development as improvement in human welfare

According to most scholars, Cuba's greatest achievement in the first three decades of the Revolution was the construction of a system that to this day provides universal free access to education, healthcare and social security: human welfare, broadly defined. The results of this system over the years are reflected in Cuba's achievement of a relatively high level of human development, particularly as measured by the UNDP in terms of life expectancy and the level of education.

In 1990, when the socialist world was collapsing and the capitalist world order was in disarray, and when Cuba was entering a system-threatening Special Period, the UNDP launched its flagship annual publication, the *Human Development Report,* designed to measure and rank countries according to their success in achieving human development. Cuba was ranked sixty-second out of 130 countries using the UNDP's human development index (HDI). Two years later, Cuba's ranking dropped to eighty-first (sixty-first in the category of "developing countries"), a clear reflection of the drastic reduction in GDP and per-capita income. In 1993, reflecting both realities in Cuba and possibly methodological irregularities, Cuba was ranked seventy-fifth on the HDI in relation to other developing countries, but 100th overall. Just a year later, Cuba's ranking returned to eighty-ninth and 108th (out of a larger group of 173 countries). In terms of the UNDP's "capability poverty" measure, Cuba ranked tenth out of all developing countries: not nearly as high as one might expect, but then the country was at the nadir of a devastating economic crisis.

From 1994 to 2000, when Cuba introduced a series of reforms designed to restructure the economy, a slow but persistent improvement in socioeconomic conditions could be detected in spite of increasing inequalities. This trend was reflected in a steady improvement in the HDI, ranking from to fifty-eighth in 1999, to fifty-sixth in 2000 and fifty-first in 2009, at last placing it in the "high human development" category.

What is most significant about this achievement in social development is that it was brought about even at a time of low economic function. While Cuba ranks very highly at the level of social development — indeed on par with the most advanced capitalist democracies — at the level of economic development it ranks among low income countries. It is worth pointing out that another state in the world has achieved this in a similar way, Kerala in India.[1]

An improvement in the social welfare of a population, an essential dimension of human development under both capitalism and socialism, is generally brought about by the agency of the state. It entails the funding of programs designed to extend essential social services to the population, especially education and healthcare, and also to ensure that everyone's basic human needs (for food, housing, health, etc.) are met. In the 1970s, this "basic needs" paradigm provided the policy framework and was used to shape the development model of governments within both capitalist systems (the welfare development state) and the socialist system (Cuba, for one). In capitalist systems the welfare and the development functions of the state require a redistribution of market-generated incomes by way of progressive taxation, channelling a share of these incomes into social welfare and development programs to build human capital and to ensure a modicum of social welfare.

Under a socialist system the provision of human welfare is a fundamental responsibility of the state and a matter of the highest priority. In the case of Cuba, this is clearly reflected in the constitution of the Cuban state. In this regard the socialist state can be differentiated from any capitalist state. In the capitalist model, all legal and other institutions are designed firstly to provide security to property in the means of production — and only secondly to protect the inalienable rights of each individual as well as the freedom to pursue his or her self-interest. The socialist state in contrast (as in the case of Cuba) attributes these rights and this freedom to the individual but defines them in terms of a collective concern for shared values and beliefs, a culture of solidarity, which gives a social form to individual human development.

In addition to instituting a system of human welfare provision with universal coverage of education, healthcare and social security, the welfare function of the Cuban state was instituted in the form of 1. a ration card that ensured the access of all citizens to affordable food and household needs, 2. workplace *comedores* and daycare centres and 3. legislation limiting the cost of housing and rental charges to 10 percent of earned income. In addition to these programs and this social development policy, the government from the outset promulgated legislation designed to bring about a fundamental structural change in the dominant social relations of production and consumption. The first measures taken included land reform legislation designed to resolve the problem of landlessness and rural poverty by redistributing large landholdings among the direct producers and family farmers.

Other measures included the socialization and nationalization of production and a public system that provided employment and work for all, with a relatively flat or egalitarian payscale that allowed for a more equitable distribution of earned income. Zimbalist and Brundenius (1989) calculate that by 1965 the wage differential ratio between the highest and lowest groups of paid workers in the payscale was 4.3 to 1, as against an estimated ratio of 25 to 1 prior to the Revolution. Mesa-Lago calculates that the payscale differential was further reduced from 3.6 to 1 in 1966, to 2.6 to 1 in 1971 (Mesa-Lago, 2000: 225). Given that the income of most Cubans was regulated by means of this payscale (the only source of income at the time), the levelling effect of the government's push towards a more egalitarian society is evident.

Table 2.1 provides a snapshot of the social conditions resulting from these and other policy measures achieved in twenty-five years. The figures in the table are averages. However, the universal coverage of the welfare system and the lack, in Cuba, of fundamental class divisions in the distribution of wealth and income that is characteristic of other countries in the region and the capitalist world mean that the social conditions indicated by figures here are highly generalized. Unlike other countries in the region, there is no poverty and wealth at the extremes of the income distribution in Cuba.

Table 2.1 Conditions of human development in 2009, expressed in averages

	Cuba	U.S.	U.K.
Life expectancy	78.5	79.1.	79.3
Infant mortality	5	8	6
Doctors per capita	1:160	1:280	–
Literacy	100%	97%	99%
Unemployment	1.9%	5%	4.7%
Poverty	0	12%	17%

Source: UNDP (2009); Save the Children (2010); World Health Organization (2007); ONE, Cuba's Office of National Statistics (2006).

A study published in the December 2005 MEDICC *Review* shows Cuba at the top of all Latin American countries in providing the greatest opportunities for human development and the elimination of avoidable unjust inequalities (unlike the UNDP, whose HDI does *not* take into account social inequalities in the human condition). This MEDICC *Review* study is based on statistics and reports published by the UNDP, the World Health Organization (WHO) and the Food and Agricultural Organization of the United Nations (FAO) and on data from related regional organizations that have studied longevity, literacy, access to safe drinking water, the student-teacher ratio, physicians per inhabitant, environmental protection and other indicators. "The combination of free and universal healthcare and education, public participation, and the willingness by the government to implement policies to maximize equity, has had positive effects on health outcomes," the MEDICC *Review* article explained. One of these outcomes had to do with infant mortality, which the WHO takes as an important "thermometer" of social well-being. This thermometer showed Cuba with 5.6 deaths per 1,000 live births, compared, for example, to the U.S., where in 2005 infant mortality stood at 6.5 (14.5 deaths for babies of African-American parents), and in 2010 the U.S. ratio was 8:1,000 (Save the Children, 2010). In Cuba, it is fair to say, there is no evident colour distinction in health conditions and healthcare. Other indicators were as follows:

- the under-five mortality rate was 7.7 per 1,000. This was better than averages in the "most developed" or "advanced" countries and indicated the best performance of all "developing" countries (89–161);
- 99 percent of births are attended by professional staff;
- Only 5.5 percent of babies are low-birth weight; and
- Cuba has one of the fastest aging populations (15.4 percent are over sixty years old) but instead of government cutting back on old age benefits, as is happening in so many capitalist "democracies," in Cuba, these benefits were increased. In 2005, the minimum pension was raised by another 50 percent.

Socialist human development as equality, freedom and solidarity

Human development in its social liberal variant, that is, as predicated on capitalism as the operating system, has three essential dimensions: economic, political and social. The economic dimension is measured in terms of per-capita income, access to which is critical in capitalist societies, in which most people have to work for a living. The social dimension relates to education and health, both of which allow individuals to live a life that they have reason to value and to realize their full human potential. The political dimension relates to Amartya Sen's concept of "development as freedom," that is to say, the ability and freedom of individuals to take advantage of opportunities for their self-advancement, or "the enlargement of choices and opportunities." This is also presented in the mainstream development discourse as equity or equality of opportunity. In the original conception of human development embodied in the HDR, there is no measure of social equality or of development as a condition given to all. As noted earlier, the HDI measures the social condition of individuals as a statistical average within the population as a whole. Needless to say, in a class-divided society, in which wealth and income tend to be concentrated — with a small group of super-rich, or the top 1 percent, appropriating the lion's share of the nation's wealth (up to 40 percent in the case of the U.S. today)[2] — this statistical average has no meaning.

In a socialist system, however — at least, in principle or in the case of Cuba — it is entirely different. Each dimension of the human development process (equality, freedom, solidarity) is understood in terms of conditions that are "equal for all," conditions that cut across "intersections of social inequalities" or, "multiple sources of disadvantage, such as class, gender, caste, race, ethnicity," in short, all those things that militate against human development (G. Sen, Iyer & Mukherjee, 2009). Thus, unlike capitalist human development, socialist *human* development is measured in terms of the degree to which this condition of equality is truly achieved.

Conclusion

The most surprising feature of developments in Cuba from 1959 to 1989 was the level of human development in terms of social welfare achieved with relatively low levels of per-capita GDP and sluggish rates of economic growth. Throughout the 1960s and 1970s the Revolutionary regime struggled to maintain some equilibrium between economic growth and social development. It managed to sustain a steady advance in social development; its policies were reflected in a steady improvement in the social conditions of Cubans. However, the regime did not manage to find a steady hand at the helm of economic growth, which experienced dramatic swings over these two decades. While economic growth fluctuated wildly, the key indicators of human development, particularly in health and education, but also in employment and housing, point towards a significant and steady improvement in social welfare, not just for certain groups but for the population generally. Normally — or rather, in development theory — indicators of economic and social development are closely correlated, the second generally tracking the first. But in Cuba this is not so. And there can be no doubt as to the agency of this development. Rather than prioritizing economic growth and making the misguided assumption that economic growth will inevitably or naturally (following the filter-down theory) bring with it an improvement in social conditions (from the workings of the market), the Revolutionary regime placed social development as its first priority and used the agency of the state to bring it about. This conclusion has far-reaching implications for human development theory, which is to say the importance of public action and the role of the state.

Not that another conclusion could not be drawn from these findings. The failure of the Cuban economy to achieve a take off rate of economic growth might well be interpreted by economists and policy-makers (those working within the orthodox paradigm of economic development) to mean that there is an inevitable trade-off between growth and distribution, and that in consideration of the higher rates of economic growth achieved by regimes that prioritized growth over distribution, a "growth first" policy could be justified both theoretically and programmatically. The response that this author would make to this (on the basis of findings and a Cuban Revolution perspective) is to ask how development is conceived and what the priorities of the government are. Are these priorities oriented towards economic growth, the fruits of which are very unevenly distributed? Or are they oriented to advance the level of human development under conditions of increased social equality?

Another conclusion that that can be drawn from our findings is that — in the context of the economic model that was used to guide economic and social policy throughout the developing world — the strategy pursued by the Cuban government could well be described, as Beatriz Díaz (1992) did, as one designed to produce "growth with equity." Of course, Cuba was not the only government at the time to pursue a growth-with-equity strategy. The government of India's Kerala State certainly did (within the framework of a communist party regime), as did governments in nation-states such as Sri Lanka and Costa Rica, and in these latter cases this was worked out as part of capitalist economic regimes. What this strategy meant was an orientation of the government's fiscal resources and expenditures towards an investment in people and towards social infrastructure (human capital formation) as well as towards productive transformation and economic growth. It also meant that economic growth was included in the mix of human development policies, that efforts were made to ensure an equitable distribution of this growth and that the government was the agency of these efforts. As for economic growth, it is evident that governments have a role to play, but this case study of Cuba does not address the broader questions at the centre of the economic development debate. It does address the preferred relationship between the public and private sector and how a balance can be achieved between the role of the market and the role of the state as well as that of a civil society.

3. Socialism as Revolutionary Consciousness

La conciencia (revolutionary consciousness) is an attitude of struggle, dignity, principles and revolutionary morale.

— *Fidel Castro, 1980, in Blum, 2011:5*

Revolution is a sense of the historic moment; it is changing everything that should be changed; it is complete equality and freedom; it is being treated and treating others like human beings; it is emancipating ourselves through ourselves, and through our own efforts; it is defying powerful dominating forces inside and outside the social and national sphere; it is defending values that are believed in at the cost of any sacrifice: modesty, selflessness, altruism, solidarity and heroism; it is fighting with audacity, intelligence and realism; it is never to violate fundamental ethical principles; it is the profound conviction that there is no force in the world capable of crushing the strength of truth and ideas.

— *Fidel Castro, May Day Address, May 1, 2000*

From the outset a defining feature of the Cuban Revolution was a manifest concern to break from, first, a capitalist-induced culture of material consumption and, second, from the pursuit by each and every individual of their own interest. The Revolution hoped to replace these capitalist approaches with a new socialist ethic of social solidarity, an ethic that required, according to Che Guevara, "the formation of an *hombre nuevo*, 'a new man and a new woman,'" which, he stressed, could only happen in the revolutionary process of creating a new society (Guevara, 2006). As both Marx and Guevara emphasized, people must become other than what they are, or rather, other than what they have become. They must be transformed in the process of struggle, changed through "the progressive formation of new values" (Castro, 1992). This struggle, Fidel emphasized, requires a veritable cultural revolution that would generate a revolutionary socialist consciousness that each person is a social being, part of a larger whole, and must act in solidarity with others, motivated by a "love of humanity" (Guevara, 1965 [2005]).

A consistent theme in Marx's political writings was the need for revolutionary practice: the simultaneous changing of people's circumstances and of themselves. By struggling against capital to satisfy their collective needs, workers transform themselves in such a way as to prepare them for a new society. They come to recognize the nature of the system and to recognize that they cannot limit themselves to guerrilla wars against the effects of the existing system, but that they need collectively to act in changing the system, transforming both society and themselves in the process. And that consciousness, Marx recognized, was the element that capitalism could not tolerate without collapse.

The objective conditions of revolutionary transformation would be created by a development of the forces of production to the point at which they could no longer be expanded on the basis of existing relations. However, a process of revolutionary transformation also has subjective conditions: it requires a population that is conscious of the need to change society and that recognizes its own power to bring about that change, that sees itself as the agent of revolutionary change. However — and this for Che Guevara was the paradox of social change — this revolutionary consciousness and the creation of a new society also required the new men and the new women just as the creation of these new human beings required a new society.

As Che Guevara understood Marx, the revolutionary process was itself a fundamental crucible of change, creating the necessary conditions for revolutionary transformation: a revolutionary (or socialist) consciousness of the need for change, and the creation of a class of new individuals committed and schooled in struggle and disposed to bring it about. This meant constant struggle and "education," "self-education" and militant action in the service of one's fellow human beings.

As for the agency of revolutionary change — the transformation of society and, in the process, the creation of "new human beings" or "new people" — it is made up of a revolutionary vanguard of the most committed members invested with a love of humanity, a leadership cadre armed with revolutionary consciousness.

The first task of the Revolutionary leadership is, in the words of Fidel Castro, "to arm people's minds, arm their minds! Not even physical weapons can avail them if their minds have not been well armed first" (November 29, 1971). The second task is to establish the Revolutionary government, a government committed to mobilizing the people on behalf of the policies that meet the needs of the people and that lead them to the greatest realization of human potential. Here the essential issue (see the discussion below on cultural revolution) is the capacity or the degree to which the government is able to free the population from a culture of possessive individualism and consumerism and the ideological dominion of capital.

Only with this emancipatory praxis can the leadership cadre hope to prioritize and facilitate human development — which is to say, the development of human needs and capacities by means of the transformation of the forces of production. This is the first task. The second is brought about by means of public action, the combination of state and popular power vested in the Local Bodies of People's Power (OLPP) within the state apparatus. Using this means, the second task is to bring about the revolutionary transformation of society and the people that make it up (the new human beings). This means a radical transformation of that society in which the owners of the means of production were in a position to enrich themselves by exploiting the labour of others and were able, in the process, to appropriate an undue share of the social product. A revolutionary transformation would bring about a new society in which all individuals could overcome their alienation and fully realize their human potential. This would be a society advanced by a revolutionary government with the active mobilized support of the people under conditions of human development. What is needed above all, according to Che Guevara, is a cultural revolution: the creation of new people freed from a concern for self-interest and instead, committed to the new society (Guevara, 1965 [2005]). The agency of this revolutionary change, he added, is both a committed leadership and active social participation. As for the forces of change in this agency, they include education, self-education, liberated labour and above all, participation in the struggle for revolutionary change.

Shaping of a revolutionary consciousness: Education and struggle

It is clear that the leaders of the Cuban Revolution were convinced that a new society based on justice and solidarity would require above all a cultural revolution: a profound transformative change in values. This change could then rebuild the concerns that motivated people in their everyday lives and in their individual and collective actions as social beings. Che Guevara was very insistent on the need for a cultural revolution as a condition of socialist human development. As he saw it, a revolutionary consciousness had to be forged based on a socialist ethic of human development and on a new society in which the socialist ideals of freedom and equality were both reinstitutionalized and realized. For Che Guevara this meant making a fundamental break from the capitalist culture of possessive individualism and bringing about a social and cultural transformation by means of education, both self-education and mass organization, and thus the mobilization of the people in support of the Revolution.

Upon achieving power the revolutionaries realized that the process of creating a revolutionary consciousness had only just begun, and that the revolutionary struggle — an essential condition for shaping revolutionary consciousness on a national level — would continue. What this meant — particularly for Guevara, who with Castro was a chief theorist and ideologue of the Revolution — was education and a process of mass mobilization designed to engage the population in a fundamentally different ethic and ethos. Engagement in the struggle, Guevara argued, was itself an important condition of self-education as consciousness grew of the need for a new society that would be capable of meeting the material and spiritual needs of all members of society. And indeed, the revolutionary struggle for power in Cuba had already brought about some of the objective and subjective conditions of such a development: the potential for revolutionary transformation. However, once power was achieved the problem of realizing this potential emerged — a problem, according to Che Guevara, of self-education and figuring out how to engage the struggle in this changed power-context.

In India's Kerala State, access to education and the institution of a public education system accessible to all — particularly the hitherto excluded lower castes — was a major demand of the social reform movements that brought a truly socialist human development regime to power. But in Cuba, education (both self-education in the process of collective struggle and the formal education system set up by the Revolutionary regime) was intrinsically linked to the goal of transforming Cubans into new people — and empowering them to participate actively in the revolutionary process of creating a new society, transforming themselves in the process. At the beginning, the public system of education had little to do with any policy or plan for economic development. As already discussed, it had to do with creating conditions that would allow Cubans from all walks of life to realize their full human potential.

Education for human development
In addition to organizing one of the best and free public school systems anywhere, Cuba captured the world's attention, just two years into the Revolution, for its innovative and revolutionary nine-month literacy campaign which mobilized 100,000 secondary students and other volunteers to impart the skills of reading and writing to 707,000 adults in all parts of the country. A notable aspect of this mass participation, which was especially important in healthcare, was the pivotal role of women's agency. Not surprisingly, today women make up nearly half of all physicians as well as directors of hospitals and polyclinics (Mehrotra, 2000:402).

In the 1950s, and even in the 1960s, women's situation was quite different regarding their active participation in social life and public decision-making, and in terms of their empowerment to act in the collective interest. The same applies to the urban and rural poor, who, prior to the Revolution, suffered from extreme social exclusion. They were unable actively to participate in decision-making about critical conditions of their lives and livelihoods. The Revolution, because it encouraged participation in the process of revolutionary transformation at the level of these mass literacy and educational campaigns, had a powerful liberating effect on the poorest people in Cuba.

These campaigns may be regarded as one of the many pivotal and symbolic moments in the path travelled by Cubans in their cultural revolution. As Che Guevara conceived it, the revolutionary reconstruction of consciousness from capitalist to socialist values entailed an enriched educational process.

One of the agencies set up by the government to implement this strategy was the Escuela al Campo (School in the Countryside, or EAC). The EAC was specifically and purposely created as a space to secure revolutionary values among young people when they were searching for their individual identities (Ministry of Education 1992:1). The Cuban Ministry of Education calls the EAC "an incubator for revolutionary commitment," serving to instill revolutionary citizenship values of hard work, sacrifice, patriotism, equality, anti-imperialism, responsibility, collectivism and solidarity with the proletariat. This incubation could instill a revolutionary consciousness and socialize new generations of Cubans into socialist values of human development, converting some key values into organizational principles and a cultural tradition of revolutionary change. *La conciencia,* for Guevara, was clearly denoted in the English translation "consciousness" or "awareness." It entailed a commitment to action forged in a process of political education and active participation in revolutionary struggle (Guevara, 2006). It was during this time that Fidel Castro defined *la conciencia* as, "an attitude of struggle, dignity, principles and revolutionary morale" (cited in Blum, 2011:5).

The idea of the EAC was based on previous successes in using generalized mobilization in the countryside to raise the level of consciousness. The leadership recognized that a revolutionary consciousness, "could not be developed merely by means of propaganda or indoctrination but must arise fundamentally from revolutionary praxis" (Medin, 1990:6). This consciousness had to arise from an active participation in militant armed struggle or other such action and mobilizations. In the 1950s, the Rebel Army in the Sierra Maestra gained the support of *campesinos* by teaching them literacy skills. The 1961 Literacy Campaign — sowing *la conciencia,* as Castro and Guevara conceived of it (on this see Fernandéz, 2000) — resulted not only in a profound attachment to new socialist ideals and the values embedded in the Revolution but also resulted in an ideological commitment to the Revolution on both cognitive and political levels. As noted by the Cuban intellectual José Antonio Portuondo, "the young literacy teachers discovered their country, and in a year of direct experience, of immediate contact with the oppressed of country and city, they earned their degrees as revolutionaries and were ready to effect a radical transformation in the unjust social order" (1980:17) The new Latin American left at the time was familiar with this process of transformation as *"concientization"* ("making conscious" or "consciousness-raising") or as "politicization." Cubans called it *la conciencia.*

By 1966, the EAC became a major focus of Cuban education policy (Blum, 2008). As noted by Blum in her review of the EAC experiment,[1] its aims were clearly defined. "It was to produce a new kind of citizen, imbued with the love of ... country, ready for [revolutionary change and committed] ... to increasing the wealth of the community, realizing the value of labour and prizing it." More specifically, Blum added, the EAC aimed to reduce or overcome the disparity between town and country, to establish close links between school and life, to educate the rising generation for work by actually working and, in line with a common objective, to demand the highest possible standards while respecting the personality of the pupils (Araujo, 1976:12).

The Revolutionary government placed a high value on relating study and work in a humanizing process of productive labour. In a formulation that owes much to Marx, the Cuban conception of education emphasized the holistic development of a new socialist citizen, to be achieved by formal and self-education programs that involved students in a process of productive labour, and workers in lifelong study and reflection. The integration of study and work schedules was later abandoned as practical productive labour continued to form an important part of the school curriculum. Teachers were expected to plan their lessons ahead of time to accommodate a designated month of agricultural service. Indeed it was deemed to be their revolutionary duty to encourage and recruit as many students as possible for this voluntary service.

As a participant-observer, Blum relates what she saw, and gives an account of the interviews and surveys from her experience in a Cuban Escuela al Campo, located on a collective farm outside Havana. Los Pioneros (Pioneers), the youth section of the official Cuban Communist Party, continue to organize the EAC program nationwide to this day. The program's rugged, military lifestyle experience is required for all city-based junior high school students in Cuba and is an essential rite of passage in the politicization and socialist consciousness-raising efforts of the Revolutionary government. Blum in this connection argues that beneath the revolutionary symbols and activities of the EAC, a new and latent socialist consciousness has evolved for some time, one that reflects neither an absolute nor an erosion of socialist ideals.

As Blum constructs it, the forming of a socialist consciousness is a matter of education. The school curriculum itself in many ways prepares students for the EAC. For example, she notes that in mathematics textbooks, the word problems use the agricultural contexts for learning arithmetic. In the civic education textbooks, *el amor al trabajo* (the love of work) is a prominent theme; young people are portrayed as heroes in different types of work, including daily life, defending *la patria* (the homeland), in construction, sports, education and culture. One photo shows a teenager aiming an AK–47 and others depict young people actively engaged in productive work. Under the pictures are statements such as "the defense of the socialist patria is the greatest honour and the supreme duty of every citizen"; "Work in socialist society is a right, a duty and a motive of honour for every citizen"; and "Voluntary work, the cornerstone of our society" (Blum, 2008).

This use of education as an instrument of consciousness-raising was a key tactic in the Revolution's human development strategy. As early as July 1960, the Fuerzas Armadas Revolucionarias (Revolutionary Armed Forces, or FAR) and the Dirección Nacional de las Militias (National Directorate of Militias) began to train civilian instructors who were to "give revolutionary talks in their respective militias, unions [and] work centres," so as to "create true revolutionary consciousness in the men and women who form their endless ranks" (*Verde Olivo*, July 1960, cited in Medin, 1997: 1). The same approach was taken in preparations for the 1961 literacy campaign. In this campaign, the materials to be used were carefully designed to adjust the context to the standpoint and realities lived and understood by the illiterate rural and urban poor. Many poor people in the cities were recent migrants from the countryside. In the preparation of these materials, according to a UNESCO report on the subject (Medin, 1990:8), teachers studied tape-recorded conversation guides to ascertain "not only the idiom of the illiterate but also his social and economic viewpoint." The actual content of the curriculum was designed (as theorized and projected by the Brazilian educator Paulo Freire) to lead students to understand the realities of their social existence, to make them aware and to empower them to act. In this context, illiterate people were taught not only how to read and write, they were taught the language of revolution.

The Special Period (officially from 1996 to 2004) was marked by a new notion of the ideal citizen with a socialist consciousness: the *hombre novísimo*, literally an "even newer socialist man." During the Revolutionary period from 1959 through the 1970s, the ideal Cuban citizen was a person with the humility and stamina of the *campesino* combined with the education, ideology and commitment of a revolutionary. During the Special Period, the Communist Party, shorn of any role in the public process of democratic elections, but continuing as a vanguard organization assigned primary responsibility for maintaining ideological commitment to the Revolution, began to idealize a new kind of Cuban citizen — the even newer person, who was urban and educated, but who nevertheless retained a *campesino* morality and soul, and remained profoundly Cuban in his or her identity. This new person was still a communist in his or her modesty and loyalty, and still a revolutionary in his or her love of humanity, but less aligned with a political party and more inspired by the philosophy of José Martí. The *hombre novísimo* had an even stronger sense of national patriotism and of unity with all Latin American and world-wide struggles against imperial domination.

The concern behind this notion of the even newer person was to rescue Cubans from the growing threat of a capitalist pseudo-culture, of alienating consumerism and possessive individualism, and to defend the Revolution from the forces of neoliberal globalization. The EAC was again pressed into service as a mechanism of acculturation, a means of combating the disease of capitalism (the virus of consumerism) and "resurrecting the authentic soul of Cuba" (Blum, 2008).

In order to understand the way in which the EAC served to form the *hombre novísimo*, Blum studied the self-reported views of parents and the youth involved in the EAC. What she found was a "dialogic and hybrid quality" present in the way parents and youth thought about and rationalized the EAC experience. As she represents this finding — somewhat problematically, it has to be said — parents and youth saw the EAC program as "both meaningful and important and meaningless and unimportant." For example, the parents, according to Blum, harbour anger and resentment that the state did not provide the necessary resources for them to participate in the program, but that the state spun "empty promises" that "hard work would bring material abundance for all." The problematic aspect of this formulation is that it is most unlikely that the state, in any of its personifications, would possibly argue that hard work would bring about material abundance for all. The author presents no evidence in this regard. It would be highly contradictory to fight and counter a capitalist culture of consumerism with a promise of abundance for all.

More convincing is Blum's account of the way that the EAC in its structure served to reinforce a socialist culture of substantive equality, that is, of an equality not so much of opportunity — which in many contexts is reduced to an abstract right without reality — but more of equality as a widely shared social condition. The problem here was a disjunction between the experience created by the EAC, which is one of sharing, and the conditions in Cuban society created by policy responses to the economic crisis. The structure of the EAC equalized and sometimes inverted relations of inequality and social hierarchy and brought about many shared experiences. Also, the collective work experience of the EAC tended to blur social distinctions. The provision of community service in the countryside also helped to break down barriers between intellectual and manual forms of labour, between the countryside and city, between the *campesino* or farmer and the urban professional, between the working and middle classes.

Most important in terms of rebuilding a socialist ethic and a revolutionary consciousness in conditions of economic crisis, the EAC experience, in Blum's findings, fosters an atmosphere of "empathy, love, humbleness and service to and with the *campesinos*." Blum found that the EAC experience encouraged students to think independently (from their parents) and to take on leadership roles, including participation in self-government, becoming brigade leaders and barrack inspectors. In many instances emulation, a socialist type of competition, existed in most camp activities. Emulation involved not only recognition of exemplary workers but recognition that one only became exemplary when one helped others to succeed. Under conditions of the Special Period, intense emotional and physical engagement and investment in a rural, rugged area was conducive and perhaps fundamental to nurturing a socialist and revolutionary consciousness and passionate civic commitments.

4. Solidarity as a
Pillar of Cuban Socialism

Solidarity in the heart of a people is impossible without solidarity among all peoples.

— Fidel Castro

To bring about a better society and progress at the level of social welfare rather than economic growth, the French revolutionaries called for freedom, equality and solidarity. The U.S. revolutionaries similarly called for a system that would secure the right of each member of society the freedom to pursue the inalienable human right to the pursuit of happiness. To bring about progress so conceived, the U.S. revolutionaries entrenched in their new constitution the formal equality of each individual in the face of the law and the eyes of God. Each individual was to enjoy a number of fundamental human rights, including the freedom of expression and political organization, and to be protected in these rights. What the United States Constitution did not guarantee was that these rights would be given and secured by the state under conditions of social solidarity, which is to say, in conditions that were equal for all. And that this was not guaranteed was quite deliberate. The American state was founded on the principle of private property in the means of social production, thus guaranteeing the legal right of the owners of property freely to dispose of it in their own economic interest. For this reason, the United States and other democratic states and capitalist economies — capitalist democracies — were constituted so as to give institutional form to the principle of freedom, which gave priority to economic and political freedom over social equality and solidarity in the scale of values. The resulting system and subsequent regimes were democratic in form but class-based and class-divided, resulting in conditions of substantive social inequality in access to the means of social production and the distribution of the social product. Under these conditions social solidarity is simply not possible.

Solidarity, as a value and organizational principle, refers to a condition in which all members of society are bound together by relationships of social support and mutual obligation: a community spirit of sharing and belonging. It is predicated on relative equality of social conditions: an egalitarian society based on the absence of class-based or structured inequalities and, in the Cuban context, the construction of a new person and the effective presence of cooperative economic and social activity. It is most often realized in relatively small societies characterized by communalism or communitarian social relations, that is to say, societies constituted as a community of relative equals. Notoriously, such a society in which people are bound by a sense of solidarity was a casualty of the process of productive and social transformation, and class formation, required by capitalist development.

In the modern world of capitalist development and liberal democracy — especially in the United States — social solidarity, in the words of Joseph Schwartz (2009), is the "forgotten sibling" among the family of three democratic values, "liberty, equality and fraternity," that have suffused democratic social revolutions from the French Revolution onwards. While school children in the U.S. are taught that the American Revolution fought for the rights to "life, liberty and the pursuit of happiness" — or "the pursuit of property," according to British philosopher John Locke — the less liberal-individualist and more democratic-collectivist French Revolution spoke of "liberty, equality and fraternity." The concept of fraternity or solidarity implies that, in the course of constructing the enterprise of creating a better form of society and a more human form of development, people develop a capacity for empathy and trust in their fellow beings — a sense of social solidarity, we would say today, or as Che Guevara would have said, a "love of humanity."

In capitalist or other class-based forms of society that are governed by hierarchical norms of class and status, social obligations and duties are fixed in customary practice and cultural tradition. In contrast, in community-based societies, such obligations and duties are based on a consciously chosen practice of solidarity, which in turn is based on a system in which relations and conditions are relatively egalitarian and are shared in the interests of democratic or social justice. In these communities in other relatively egalitarian societies — even in the welfare states and social liberal democracies of Europe — the polity collectively regulates the social relationships established by economic and social life (Schwartz, 2009:27).

Thus, all democratic societies, at a minimum — with the U.S. a possible exception — are at least *nominally* committed to ensuring that citizens are not so destitute or socially marginalized that they cannot meet their basic needs or participate in political life. Much of the ongoing struggle between the democratic Left and the Right in the class-divided but "advanced" capitalist societies, has revolved around the question of the extent to which social rights (as opposed to economic freedoms or political rights) or public provision should constrain the most non-egalitarian outcomes of a capitalist economy (including an allegedly meritocratic "modern" education system). By means of political conflict (rather than abstract philosophical argument) capitalist "democracies" have developed social policies and institutions designed to cushion individuals from the risks and vicissitudes of the capitalist marketplace. Thus, even the most illiberal of capitalist democracies, the United States, provides minimal universal insurance against disability, unemployment, abject poverty (and hunger, if not homelessness) and old age. In the words of the conservative (and "pragmatic liberal"), U.K. Tory leader David Cameron, "my government always looks after the elderly, the frail, the poorest in our country" (*New York Times*, May 17, 2010). In the light of the last thirty years of neoliberal policies, and the 33 percent of British citizens living in poverty in 2014, such claims would have to be called into serious question.[1]

The ultimate democratic trust, Schwartz argues (with particular reference to the U.S.; 2009:27), "resides in the sharing of the burden of bearing of arms to defend the nation." In the context of revolutionary socialist Cuba, it is a matter instead of defending *la patria* from U.S. imperialism. As for international solidarity (and the right to human or social development) — the principle of which is codified in the Cuban Constitution — the issue is support for the struggles of people all over the world against oppression and exploitation. Specifically, Article 12 of the Cuban Constitution states that "the Republic of Cuba espouses the principles of anti-imperialism and internationalism." And section d of Article 12 adds that Cuba "advocates the unity of all third world countries in the face of the neocolonialist and imperialist policy which seeks to limit and subordinate the sovereignty of our peoples, and worsen the economic conditions of exploitation and oppression of the underdeveloped nations."

Underlying this principle of solidarity is the notion of moral (and instrumental) duty and readiness of all members of society (both in Cuba and the world) to ensure the well-being of the collectivity and to share more equitably in the product of collective economic enterprise. Political theorists have long debated whether such an impulse derives from a universal human inclination to aid those less fortunate than ourselves (charity) or from human engagement in activities that construct social bonds of mutual support among the members of societies "on the road to economic and political integration for the attainment of true independence" (Cuba, Constitution, Article 12d). The classic example of such an ethic is the shared burden of work symbolized by the trade union motto, "an injury to one is an injury to all." A more contemporary example is found in Subcomandante Marcos' declaration that no one is free while some people elsewhere remain oppressed. Fidel Castro himself in this connection declared that internationalism is integral to socialist development and that true solidarity is not possible without solidarity among all peoples.

This concern for solidarity is not just a matter of theoretical debate. In Cuba it is also a matter of constitutional principle and political practice. At this level it is possible to discern major differences in the value placed on solidarity as a fundamental principle of social organization and the institutionalization of this value as a principle of revolutionary consciousness — a cultural revolution, one might argue. A culture is sustained by a complex of values and beliefs. For a value to be converted into an organizational principle it must take form as a belief that has been long held, consented to by members of society and entrenched in institutional practice. Lying somewhere between a tradition and a principle, a value suggests the kind of belief that, if seriously challenged, would overturn the prevailing worldview, something for which no law is needed because it would be freely enforced by social consensus.

Emile Durkheim, one of the founders of sociology as an academic discipline, argued that any social order is predicated on some form of social solidarity, or ties of mutual obligation and shared morality. He argued that even class-divided societies based on an extended division of labour and a high degree of individuation have a moral basis. Thus, the difference between inherently unequal class-divided societies (capitalism, for example) and societies that are more egalitarian, is not just about the mode of production and the associated social structure, but is also determined by whether the prevalent form of organization is communal or associational. On this issue there is a long-standing sociological debate about the impact of modernization on the structure of society. It has been found that modernization generally brings about a transformation in the dominant form of social organization, replacing communal forms of organization (based on norms of reciprocal exchange and a culture of social solidarity) with an associational type of organization and a modern capitalist form of society based on a rational calculus of shared self-interest and commercial transactions. Modernization has been found to promote a culture of possessive individualism and a calculation of self-interest, of class division and a social inequality that undermines solidarity.

In fact, it could be argued that social solidarity as a value is a victim of modernization, the casualty of "the great transformation" of a pre-capitalist and traditional form of agrarian society into a modern industrial capitalist system. At the same time it is evident that certain political practices and forms of development can serve to revive the spirit of community weakened by the forces of structural change. For example, the new paradigm of local development promoted by the theorists of "another development" in the 1990s is predicated on the rebuilding of a culture of social solidarity in local communities. Whether communities in this sense — as people bound together by a culture of mutual obligation and social bonds — still exist or might be found is very much at issue (Durston, 2001). The key question here is the penetration of capitalism in the countryside, with its inevitable solidarity-destroying class relations. The entire thrust of current development thinking and practice is towards the institutionalization of community-based forms of local development based on the accumulation of "social capital." This social capital is the one asset that the poor are deemed to have in abundance and is thus seen as a potential source of participatory development. This development would empower the rural poor to act for themselves in a quest to alleviate their poverty and sustain their livelihoods on the basis of "a culture and economy of solidarity" (Razeto, 1988, 1993).

It is assumed by these theorists and practitioners that capitalism, rather than socialism, provides the system requirements for this development. In Bolivia, the advent to state power of Evo Morales, the representative of a popular movement of indigenous communities, has led to a political project to create a solidarity-based national economy: to reconstruct the process of national development on a communalist model of social organization. Morales has claimed, "communalism is our political practice." As to whether this development process can or will proceed on a capitalist or a socialist path is unclear. What is clear and what will be argued in this chapter is that social solidarity is a fundamental principle of organization and human development for the Cuban Revolution.

Solidarity within the Revolution

A major difference between capitalist and socialist regimes of human development is in the fundamental value attached to social solidarity and a corresponding revolutionary consciousness on the part of the entire society. Human development in the UNDP model, and the associated discourse, is predicated on the value and organizational principle of equality, conceived of as a matter of opportunity or equity; and freedom, conceived of in the same terms, which is to say, as the capacity for individual self-realization of their capabilities. For the Cuban revolutionaries, however, the concepts of equality and freedom only acquire meaning with the implementation of policies designed to assure social solidarity: the identification and mutual support of all members of society viewed and treated as equals. Social solidarity or cohesion must grow on substantive equality within a relatively egalitarian society, that is, one based on egalitarian relations and an equality of social condition: equal access to society's productive resources and opportunities for collective development, and an equitable sharing of the product of collective labour. Inequality in this regard, when based on institutionalized practice, is fundamentally destructive of social solidarity or cohesion. In fact, this was concluded by economists from the Economic Commission for Latin America and the Caribbean (ECLAC) after reviewing Latin America's long and "bitter experience of inequality." They concluded that "it is time for equality" (ECLAC, 2010).

"Growth," the authors of this ECLAC study argued (with reference to the dominant economic development strategies pursued in Latin America over the past five decades), "has a negative effect on social inclusion and cohesion when its benefits ... [are] concentrated [on one socioeconomic class] .... As the expectations gap widens, social conflict increases and erodes the legitimacy of governments, thereby jeopardizing the sustainability of growth." They add that "[a] society that shares out educational opportunities and access to formal employment in a more egalitarian way" (that is, not as a commodity traded on the labour market) "will have a workforce with greater capabilities and will optimize both the use of those capabilities to make progress with ... the use of fiscal resources for productive investment and [for] social protection" (ECLAC, 2010:41). The authors conclude from their study of the "inequality predicament" that "[a] society which universalizes timely access to healthcare and nutrition will reduce the costs associated with disease and malnutrition, from lower productivity to sickness-related expenditures."

Furthermore, they write, "[a] society with a higher level of equity will ... incur fewer costs related to ... the quality of democracy" (41). They could have added (which they did in another part of the study without being explicit) that social equality is a fundamental principle of human development.

It was in this study that the ECLAC theorists declared that it was "time for equality," after five decades under conditions of state-led and then market-friendly national development. The Cuban revolutionaries had come to this same conclusion at the beginning of the development process, as the result of the revolutionary struggle itself. It was very early in Cuba's revolutionary process that the decision was made to give the land back to the "tiller" and to socialize the means of production, to secure a relative equality of income distribution via the mechanism of a relatively flat payscale for different categories of work and social contributions, to universalize access to essential public services for human welfare and development and to "share... out educational opportunities and access to formal employment."

International solidarity: Human development as the export of human capital

"Before focusing hopeful eyes on the future, you must be grounded in reality. And the reality of international cooperation is fundamentally perverse, and that's why it must be changed" (Ximena de la Barra, International Consultant, United Nations). "This," Fidel Castro has declared, "is the battle of solidarity against egoism."

The Preamble of Cuba's Constitution includes a commitment to "proletarian internationalism, on the fraternal friendship, aid, cooperation and solidarity of the peoples of the world." In Cuba's 2004 report to the United Nation's Millennium Development Goals (adopted in 2000 by 189 heads of state), it demonstrated that it had met three of the eight humanitarian goals designed with the intention of eliminating extreme poverty by 2015, and that it was on track with all the other goals. Cuba's foreign policy is, in fact, based upon the eighth goal, "to develop a global partnership for development."

In 2006, 25,000 of the nation's 70,000 doctors and several thousand other medical personnel were serving in sixty-eight countries, and a similar number of teachers and technicians were serving the cause of Cuban internationalism in a total of a hundred countries. In 2008, 38,524 Cuban healthcare workers (including 17,697 doctors) served this cause in seventy-three countries (Saney, 2009).

In addition to this export of human capital on these "internationalist missions," 27,235 young people from 120 countries are now studying in Cuba, with 80.6 percent of them intent on becoming general practitioners in the areas of greatest need in their countries. Since 1961, Cuba has graduated 45,352 medical students from 129 countries (66.4 percent from sub-Saharan Africa and 19.2 percent from eighteen Latin American countries).

Cuba is building a medical university in Venezuela, and over the last three decades it has built such centres in Equatorial Guinea, Ethiopia, Uganda, Ghana, Gambia, Yemen, Guinea Bissau, Guyana and Haiti.

In addition to providing healthcare and education, thousands of Cubans are also working abroad to assist twenty-four of the most underdeveloped nations of the world with technical advice and aid to HIV victims. In June 2001, the U.N. General Assembly met to discuss AIDS. Cuba offered doctors, teachers, psychologists and other specialists needed to assess and collaborate with the campaigns to prevent HIV and other illnesses. Cuba also offered diagnostic equipment and kits necessary for the basic prevention programs and retroviral treatment for 30,000 patients. All this was done without charge, proposing to pay the salary of these professionals in its national currency. Under pressure from the U.S., the offer was rejected with "democracy" taking precedence over health. Nevertheless, eight African and six Latin American countries accepted Cuba's AIDS intervention project, which offered education programs, the treatment of 200,000 patients and the training of half a million health workers.

The export of human capital, as the Cuban government characterizes these missions, is generally provided to individual recipient-states free of charge. In most cases, however, the states that receive aid from Cuba do pay in some form, such as by bartering oil, other resources or manufactured products.

Cuba's commitment to serving the poor, the sick and victims of natural catastrophes is a glaring contrast to the typical response of the U.S. government, even to the human disaster caused in August 2005 by Hurricane Katrina in New Orleans and Mississippi and Alabama. In this case Cuba immediately offered to help save survivors with a specially formed Henry Reeves International Team of Medical Specialists in Disasters and Epidemics. Fifteen hundred medical professionals offered to commit themselves to assist Katrina's victims, each equipped with a fifty-pound package of medicines, or a total of thirty-six tonnes of medical supplies and field hospital equipment. These missionaries had an average of ten years' clinical experience and had served in forty-three countries. But the George W. Bush regime did not even have the decency to reply to Cuba's humanitarian offer. Instead, it absorbed the loss of eighteen hundred people who died simply for lack of aid and treatment.

Henry Reeves teams were instead sent to aid Pakistani earthquake victims and Guatemalans affected by Hurricanes Stan and Wilma. Most of the 2,500 doctors and paramedics served for six months in Pakistan. By April 2006, they had treated 1.5 million patients — 73 percent of whom had been hit by one of these disasters. They had performed 13,000 surgical operations, trained 660 Pakistani medics and handed over the thirty-two field hospitals they brought with them. The Cuban government donated 241 tonnes of medicines and surgical instruments and 275 tonnes of hospital equipment during these three disasters.

The Cubans were most noted for taking on the toughest assignments, climbing in mountainous areas and working with the poorest of the poor who had never been visited by a doctor. Dictator Pervez Musharraf, a close ally and friend of George W. Bush, officially thanked Cuba and acknowledged that it had sent more disaster aid than any other country, including the United States.

In 2006, Henry Reeves volunteers numbered three thousand. They were required to speak at least two languages and be competent in epidemiology. The mission's namesake was a U.S. Civil War veteran who served in Cuba's first war of independence from Spain. Reeves, a New Yorker, earned the rank of brigadier general. He died in battle, in 1876, after having fought in four hundred battles. The MEDICC Review in the summer of 2005 explained that "recognition of Cuban expertise in disaster preparedness and response" prompted the U.N. Development Programme and Association of Caribbean States to select Havana as headquarters for the new Cross Cultural Network for Disaster Risk Reduction, which would facilitate regional cooperation in disaster management.

In 2004, Cuban doctors began to perform a simple surgery created by their associate scientists that cures many forms of blindness within two to three days. By mid-2006, a quarter of a million people, in twenty-four countries, had been cured of cataracts, retractile disorders, corneal glaucoma, myopias and strabismus. Cuba had fourteen thousand doctors working in poor areas, and many conservative Venezuelan doctors complained of the free competition and refused to offer them aid. One hundred thousand Venezuelans regained their eyesight in the first year of Cuba's Operación Milagro (Operation Miracle) program.

In this situation, Fidel Castro and Hugo Chávez agreed to provide funds, medicines and medical personnel to treat those suffering from neuropathic eye afflictions caused by malnutrition. Over one million Latin Americans are affected by these afflictions annually, and the two governments planned to operate on that many patients each year over a decade. During this initiative, Cuban medical missionaries carried backpacks with hospital equipment and medicines into the most remote areas and marginalized communities in the far corners of Latin America to perform surgery. "The world has never witnessed anything equal to this health program," commented Ralph Gonsalves, Prime Minister of Saint Vincent and the Grenadines, upon landing in Havana in 2008. Gonsalves came to thank Cuba for having cured a thousand blind citizens in yet another initiative of the Operation Miracle eye program. In the case of Saint Vincent, only a few personnel at a time were able to arrive in small aircraft since there is no international airport for larger craft. So, Cuba and Venezuela agreed to build one through their Alternativa Bolivariana para los Pueblos de Nuestra América (ALBA) cooperative trade pact. Tens of thousands of blind patients from Venezuela and from Saint Vincent were transported to Havana for surgery. This air-lift program was also funded through ALBA. The largest numbers came from Venezuela but they also came from the entire South American continent and from the Caribbean. Poor blind people in the U.S. are also eligible.

From the beginning of the Revolution, Cuba's foreign policy has focused on assisting all third world countries, especially in Latin America, the Caribbean and Africa. The aim has been to help them escape foreign domination, which, Cuba argues, keeps people in poverty, ignorance and ill health. In this, it is probably the only country in the world whose foreign policy is governed by the UNDP's dictum, "International cooperation ... should be viewed not as an act of charity but as an expression of social justice, equity and human solidarity."

Conclusion

Human development in the discourse of liberalism, embodied in the UNDP's *Human Development Report*, is based on a belief in the need for institutional reform that seeks to improve conditions of freedom and equality. It is also based on the institutionalized value of freedom, understood as the right and capacity of individual members of society to flourish in the pursuit of their opportunities for self-realization. Freedom and equality, seen in a socialist framework however, is only realized properly in the context of true solidarity.

In socialist discourse, human development is based on the belief in more radical change and on a fundamental reorganization of society that allows a new person to emerge. This new cultural and social context, together with a new international solidarity, can only come about in a revolutionary process.

This is to say, in the hierarchy of socialist values, solidarity is preeminent, in that it defines or predetermines the meaning that socialists attach to freedom and equality. The value attached to solidarity as an organizing principle is embodied in the history of the Cuban Revolution, which is played out using a socialist conception of human development as an ongoing revolutionary process. In this there is a fundamental difference between the Cuban Revolution and those of Russia and China, particularly in the historic processes through which socialism was actualized in these countries in the twentieth century. Both the Russian and the Chinese Revolutions, like the French Revolution before them, have generally been regarded as social revolutions in that the process of change entailed a restructuring of both nations at the social as well as political level; a change of both the society and the state. And the organizing principle of their transformation was equality: the socialization of production and an egalitarian distribution of the social product. But in the cases of both Russia and China, the revolutions were not ongoing, nor were they based on a systematic overhaul of the cultural foundations of the society and polity, that is, the creation of a new people and of a new society based on social solidarity. There was a belated attempt in China, in the 1960s, to bring about a cultural revolution, but, as in Russia, the people were not engaged in the process as active participants under conditions of freedom. The hallmark of the Cuban Revolution and a fundamental defining feature was its concern for human development under real conditions of freedom, equality and solidarity.

5. The Equality Dimension
of Socialist Humanism

No value defines socialism as well as equality. Freedom and solidarity are critical factors: they are social conditions of socialist development, but only in certain contexts. Cuba is one. It could be argued that equality is a fundamental principle of socialist development in any and all of its forms. Equality is also a fundamental precept for capitalist human development. However, in capitalism it is transmuted into equity, that is, it is fundamental not as equality of condition but as equality of opportunity for individuals to advance themselves or realize their capabilities (UNDP, 2010). It is, therefore, recognized that capitalist societies are necessarily class-divided, with structured inequalities in social conditions, but it is assumed that human development of these societies is possible as long as individuals are free to act and take advantage of the available opportunities, and that governments ensure that there is a relatively even playing field, providing an equality of opportunity for individuals to realize their human potential, their abilities.

The problem with this liberal notion of equal opportunity is that no matter what reforms are put into place to level the playing field for all individuals, and no matter what formal rights and freedoms are accorded to each and all individuals, the conditions of institutional participation are never the same for all individuals. These conditions depend on and vary with the social class or group or gender that the individual belongs to, and they depend on the power relationships that structure and condition both the freedom of individuals and their opportunities for self-advancement. Thus in a capitalist system, whether or not the market and the drive to accumulate is regulated or controlled, the notion of an equality of opportunities is an illusion at best, and an outright sham at worst. Under socialism equality as a formal right or opportunity available to each individual is not in question. As a matter of principle and ideological commitment, equality in a socialist system is not an abstract right but a substantive condition shared by all members of society.

In Cuba, measures were instituted from the outset of the Revolution that moved the society in this direction, including a radical land reform that dramatically improved landless rural workers' access to the means of social production and sources of rural livelihood. The subsequent collectivization of agricultural production enhanced social cooperation in the production process (Kay, 1988).

Agrarian reform in Cuba also included a policy of nationalization and socialization of production in all sectors of the economy, a process that culminated in the 1968 Revolutionary Offensive against the remaining redoubts of private enterprise, all but extinguishing the private sector and replacing the market mechanism with centralized state planning.[1] From 1968, up to 83 percent of workers were employed by the state and earned income. Income for most Cubans was regulated by a payscale that set upper and lower limits to earned income, which produced — by administrative fiat — a relatively flat or egalitarian distribution of income.

The effect of this policy was evident in a dramatic reduction in existing structured social inequalities as measured by the Gini Index, used by many economists. By this measure, Cuba had achieved a level of social equality that was incomparable, certainly in the context of Latin America, the region with the most profound and extensive social inequalities in the world according to the UNDP (2010). In 1959, the Gini coefficient for Cuba was 0.57, in line with conditions found in other parts of Latin America. But Zimbalist and Brundenius calculate that by 1986 the Cuban Gini coefficient was only 0.24, signifying one of the most equitable distributions of income in the world.

Given that the distribution of income was relatively egalitarian, one's type of work no longer played a significant role in income. Given that Cubans were and are indeed free to choose their occupation due to universal access to education — the primary avenue for social mobility and occupational choice in socialist as well as capitalist systems — Cuba, by many accounts, had made a considerable advance in the project of socialist human development. However, this advance was not measured by the HDI, since it only measures statistical averages and does not account for the *distribution* of indexed conditions across the population. The main conditions measured, income, life expectancy and education, are the major institutional and policy means (according to human development theory) for enlarging the choices and expanding the opportunities available to individuals.

Even with this deficit in the UNDP's measure of human development, Cuba scored — and continues to score — very well on each dimension of development except for per-capita income. Cuba ranked in the "high human development" category (fifty-ninth out of a total of 186 countries) in the UNDP's latest ranking in which Cuba was included (UNDP, 2011). In 2009 Cuba ranked fifty-first. Were it not for the income factor, or if the UNDP were to weight income with a social distribution or equality measure (for example, the share of national income received by the poorest 40 percent), Cuba would obviously rank even higher and place in the "very high human development" category. In regard to the non-income measures of human development, Cuba ranks with those countries now categorized as having achieved a very high level of human development. For example, in terms of life expectancy at birth, Cuba fares somewhat better than the United States, at 78.3 (76 for men, 80 for women), against the U.S.'s 78.2 (75 for men, 80 for women).

Human development as equality

Whereas human development in the context of capitalism is based on the idea of individual freedom and the values and institutions attached to it, socialist human development can be seen as growing out of a fundamental social condition of equality — Marx's "conditions equal for all" (1967b) — and out of a strong and vibrant social solidarity.

Within a capitalist development policy framework, as we have seen, the idea of equality is transmuted into equity, understood not in terms of social justice in the distribution of the social product but as equality of opportunity. The economists at the World Bank and those responsible for the UNDP's *Human Development Report* are crystal clear on this point: "for development to enlarge people's opportunities they need equitable access to these opportunities" and the freedom to pursue them; "otherwise the choices available to many individuals in society (often, entire sectors) are restricted. We must emphasize that equity should be understood as equal access to opportunities, but not equal results because what one does with one's opportunities is in the sphere of individual initiatives" (UNDP, 2010: Synopsis).[2] However, socialist human development is grounded in equality as a substantive social condition shared by all: social equality in access to society's productive resources and in the distribution of income.

Socialism was conceived in such terms by Che Guevara, whose dream and vision of socialism was one of human development: to allow new types of human beings to arise who are socialized with a revolutionary spirit and a socialist consciousness. Guevara argued the need for moral rather than material incentives: that economic behaviour should be governed by a socialist ethic and a revolutionary spirit based on the love of humanity. Guevara continually stressed that a socialist economy in itself is not "worth the effort, sacrifice, and risks of war and destruction" if it ends up encouraging "greed and individual ambition at the expense of collective spirit" (cited in Kellner, 1989:62). His primary goal thus became to reform individual consciousness and values to produce workers and citizens who were more fully conscious people. Cuba's new person would be able to overcome the culture of egotism and selfishness that characterizes capitalist societies. In describing this new method of development Guevara stated that "there is a great difference between free-enterprise development and revolutionary development. In one of them, wealth is concentrated in the hands of a fortunate few, the friends of the government, the best wheeler-dealers. In the other, wealth is the people's patrimony" (Kellner, 1989: 59).

Guevara, as Minister of Industry, put his stamp on development policy from 1964 to 1969, after the Great Debate and before the lack of economic growth led the government to revert to economic orthodoxy and switch to a more pragmatic approach. During a policy shift away from Guevara's concern for social equality and towards pragmatism and economic orthodoxy, the old wage scale was seen as too egalitarian. The government abandoned Guevara's policy of moral incentives and introduced various material incentives. A wage reform in 1981 increased the wages of highly skilled labour relative to unskilled labour, rewarding both skill and productivity. Economic growth did indeed kick in but growth was halting and sporadic until the early 1980s at which time it began a steady climb, even though the rest of Latin America was mired in debt and entered a historic decade without development.

The inception of an economic downturn in 1986 led to another switch in policy, based on an effort to rectify the mistake made by deviating from a Guevarist line in macroeconomic and development policy. Although remuneration was based on the principle of "each according to their work" rather than "according to their needs," this Rectification Program (RP) had a solid egalitarian foundation in its emphasis on moral incentives, criticism of excessive differentials, denunciation of the high private-sector earnings and concern for market-generated distortions in the egalitarian distribution of incomes. In the spirit of this rectification, and with the goal of advancing egalitarianism, the government implemented a policy of expanded rationing to counter the difficulties experienced by a growing number of households to make ends meet. The government's new wage policy was used to advance egalitarianism. In 1987 the lowest rate on the wage scale was increased from 75 pesos per month to 100, from a wage/salary rate scale of 82–93 to 107, and from 95–107 to 118 (Zimbalist & Brundenuis, 1989). As a result, the ratio of the highest to the lowest wage (the fundamental source of income in Cuba) was reduced from 5.5:1 in 1981, and to 4.5:1 in 1987, and in real terms this ratio was maintained or even reduced as Cuba entered the Special Period.

The goal of the RP was to put the Revolution back on the track of Guevara's vision of socialism as human development. The means and policy instruments for advancing the Revolution in these terms increased workers' participation in economic functions and public policy; they fomented a concern for increasing productivity and output; they fought corruption and improved labour discipline; and they restored the moral impulse to social contribution (over personal advancement) and unpaid voluntary work. At a more practical level the RP was aimed at expanding social services for human development. The share of social services in the state budget — one indicator of the government's priorities — increased from 41.8 percent in 1985 to a record 45 percent in 1988: an unheard of level in the most advanced capitalist welfare states. Investments in social services rose from 17.7 percent of total investment in 1985 to 21.5 percent in 1988. Social expenditures per capita were also programed to grow, notwithstanding their already high share of fiscal resources and in spite of declining fiscal revenues due to lower rates of economic growth.

With regard to workers' participation in the making of public policy (and continuous planning) — a key objective of the rectification campaign — the PCC Congress held in 1989 heard complaints about the inadequacy of mechanisms for workers' participation in planning and that work managers (and policy-makers) tended to treat production assemblies, as well as neighbourhood assemblies and community councils, as mere formalities. This resulted in discounting the input of workers in the policy-making process. It was considered that worker contribution to policy had become formulaic and ineffective. Also questioned at the 1989 PCC Congress was the ability of workers to participate in decisions related not to the economy as a whole but to the system of labour remuneration, conditions of work and job security, as well as hiring and firing, and redeployment of workers according to management criteria of enterprise efficiency, which, some workers argued, should be balanced against workers' rights and collective decision-making power.

As for social security, entitlement conditions were relaxed for pensions: the retirement age in 1987 was reduced while pensions were increased, benefiting some 690,000 pensioners (Mesa-Lago, 1993). In this context, social security costs (including healthcare) surpassed 9 percent of GDP in 1990, the highest ever, and total security expenditures exceeded the one billion peso mark in 1986 and kept growing even into the crisis of the Special Period. The number of pensioners surpassed a million in 1990, 64 percent more than the number in 1979. Significantly, reflecting the priority given by the government to healthcare and the training of doctors and other health professionals, the number of community clinics, doctors and healthcare professionals over the years increased to the point that Cuba has come to lead the world in the access of the general population to family doctors and primary healthcare (see Table 5.1). According to the World Bank,[3] in 2010 the number of physicians per 1,000 people in Cuba was 6.7, the highest number in the world. The patient-to-doctor ratio in Cuba today is 170 while in Canada and the U.S. it is 470 and 390 respectively.[4]

Table 5.1 Doctors per 10,000 inhabitants, selected years

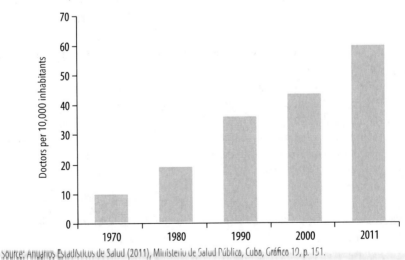

Source: Anuarios Estadísticos de Salud (2011), Ministerio de Salud Pública, Cuba, Gráfico 19, p. 151.

In terms of other indicators of human welfare, the availability and quality of consumer goods and the level of material consumption undoubtedly fell in the downturn of the second half of the 1980s, albeit under conditions of increased egalitarianism, an important indicator of socialist human development. As for education, UNESCO reported a 6 percent illiteracy rate in 1990 among those fifteen years and older. Enrolment in secondary and higher education kept increasing in this phase of Cuba's development, reaching 88 percent and 23 percent in these age groups, respectively.

Infant mortality continued its impressive fall between 1985 and 1990, a period of economic decline. Per thousand births, deaths fell from 16.5 to 10.7, exceeding the target rate of 15 by 29 percent. ECLAC reported an increase in Cuban life expectancy from 58 years in 1959, 74.3 in 1985, to 75.2 in 1990.

There are no data on social security coverage for this stage but pension expenditures increased by 44 percent. As for housing it appears that the brigades in 1986–90 built only 18,315 housing units rather than the target of 100,000. Total housing construction over the period fell, aggravating a serious housing deficit, the one most notable shortfall in the Revolution's remarkable achievements at the level of social development. This was a matter of concern in that housing generally affects health, a major condition of human development. Other shortfalls in the Revolution's achievements, or deficits in the physical quality of life, would include transportation services and access to food with regard not so much to nutrition and caloric intake as quality and range of choice. Although difficult to measure for lack of hard evidence regarding the physical quality of daily life before the onset of the production crisis between 1991 and 1993, indications are — based on anecdotal evidence and recollections by those who lived through this period — that the level of material consumption at the time was severely constrained: austere at best. This might not be seen as a major factor in determining the level of human development in terms of education and health, where the achievements of the Revolution are indisputable and well documented. However, material consumption is nevertheless an important condition of the physical quality of life.

Policy dynamics of income distribution

Economic inequalities may be defined as the differences in the distribution of income, in access to material and spiritual well-being and in consumer spending (Heller, 1999). As such, they are an expression of the different degree of resource availability and provision of means to meet the needs typical of different social groups. Within this trilogy (income, access to well-being, consumer spending), individual and family monetary income — operationally construed as the amount of money that an individual or family obtains from various sources (salaries, pensions, profits, informal sources, illegal activities, etc.) during specific periods — constitutes a primary indicator for measuring inequalities, poverty and social disadvantage.

In the case of Cuba, during the first three decades of the Revolution, structural reforms and socioeconomic changes resulted in a significant reduction of the asymmetry between both the source and distribution of monetary income. These reforms and changes led to a de-concentration of incomes (increased egalitarianism), because the most marked extremes (exploitative elites, the unemployed and those in extreme poverty) within the "stratification pyramid" were eliminated. In 1953, the richest 10 percent of the population appropriated 38 percent of total income whereas the poorest 20 percent of the population received only 2.1 percent. In 1978, only two decades on, this relationship had changed significantly: the poorest 20 percent received 11 percent of total income while the share of the richest 20 percent was reduced to 27 percent (Martínez et al., 1997).

The transition from capitalism to socialism, a process begun in the 1960s and more or less completed by 1975, entailed an expansion of the public sector in the economy and resulted in a major change in both the source and the distribution of household and individuals' incomes. The share of state employees in national income, relative to the working population as a whole, jumped from 8.8 percent in 1953 to 86 percent in 1970 and 94 percent in 1988 (Oficina Nacional de Estadísticas, 1998).

The socialization of production and nationalization of employment was accompanied by the design and implementation of a uniform and centralized wage and salary system. This new system displaced the labour market, and assumed responsibility for designing a payscale for different categories of work, establishing the upper and lower limits of earned income. The aim was to secure a more egalitarian distribution of income and to ensure equal pay for equal work. There were two main dimensions of this policy-induced improvement: earned income for public sector employment had come to represent a major source of family and individual income, and the 1983 General Salary/Wage Reform allowed only one differentiation between maximum and minimum incomes in a range from 4.5 to 1 (Nerey & Brismart, 1999). In this way the share of the poorest quintile of income earners had improved their share of total income from 2.1 to 11 percent (Martínez et al., 1997). This significant progress at the level of social equality is also reflected in the Gini Index (discussed above; Zimbalist & Brundenius 1989).

Another indicator of social equality, or egalitarianism, is the share of the lowest income earners (the bottom quintile, which in many contexts captures the rate of poverty) in total income. Arguably this is a much better measure of human development than the UNDP's measure of per-capita income, which does not measure distribution at all. Using the UNDP's scales, it is quite possible for an increase in per-capita income to be accompanied with an increase in social inequality. In terms of this critical measure of human development — the share of the bottom quintile of income earners in total national income — Cuba had made considerable progress by 1975.

At the same time, income in absolute and relative terms had become less significant as an indicator of inequality (Espina Prieto, 2005). This is because of policies pursued by the government that improved access to healthcare, education, social security, food, sports, culture and other assets and services designed to meet the basic needs of all Cubans. In effect, with the expansion of these services to most of the population, many of whom had been hitherto excluded, the relationship between material consumption or well-being and individual and family monetary income was reduced. It took a lot less personal income to provide for the population's material and spiritual needs. In any case, all indications are that the Revolutionary government made considerable progress in the direction of human development on the basis and in terms of its commitment to a policy of egalitarianism.

Gender matters: Equality at stake

According to Marta Nuñez, a Cuban sociologist working at the Centre for Studies of International Migrations at the University of Havana, a critical feature of the Cuban Revolution from the very beginning was the concerted and successful effort taken to advance the status and the increased participation of women, particularly in educational opportunities and employment (Nuñez, 2007). The resulting transformative developments, such as the feminization of the labour force, were not unlike those in other countries at the time and since. But in Cuba, there were a number of distinct permutations. For example, from the beginning, the Revolution focused on women and children, and several sections of the Cuban Constitution refer explicitly to gender equality. Indeed, the infringement of the right to equal treatment is considered a criminal offence. The Federación de Mujeres Cubanas (Federation of Cuban Women, or FMC) was founded in 1960, and it spearheaded the concerted drive to bring about a very different society in terms of social equality and egalitarian relations between men and women. In the context of the Revolution, Cuba, Nuñez emphasized, has uninterruptedly developed programs to eliminate all types of discrimination. The "struggle against gender discrimination has been one of the most successful ones, much more than those aimed at eliminating racial taboos" (2007:5).

The FMC grew from 400,000 members in 1962 to 3.2 million in 1990, and has influenced decision-making at all levels of society (Mehrotra, 2000). Indeed, Nuñez notes, by means of the FMC in particular, "women have been the engines of [many of the] transformations [wrought in Cuban society]." Among other things, the FMC promoted equal employment opportunities, maternity leave and daycare centres, and has fought indefatigably, and mostly successfully, to advance the status of women in Cuban society.

As for the broader issues of great concern to women in particular (or more so than men) the Mother-Child Health Program is an example of how the government targeted its social programs for women and children. Making children a priority can be seen, among other things, in the building of daycare centres in and near all major workplaces, the training of primary school teachers and the implementation of vaccination campaigns. The government over the years has been particularly attentive to the needs of women, children, youth and the elderly, with well over a hundred programs aimed to benefit these groups.

As Nuñez reconstructs it, programs to advance the status of women were formulated with input from two distinct but closely linked levels: that of public policies elaborated "from above" and that of responses from women's organizations to these policies. According to Nuñez, public policy proposals were seriously modified as a consequence of the women's responses. The FMC is granted special status under the Cuban Constitution and, as with all popular organizations in Cuba, reads proposed policy and initiates new legislative and policy changes.

These opportunities for influence, both from above and from below, were constituted as the result of distinct new policies, legal statutes and regulations, various economic measures, and new cultural patterns. The 1976 Constitution codified the government's public concern with women's rights: women's equal rights in marriage, employment, earnings and education. Discrimination on the basis of gender was made punishable by a withholding of ration rights and imprisonment.

The new institutional and policy framework put in place by the Revolution included a new Family Code which established maternity leave within the Labour Code, and granted free education from primary to postgraduate levels. It brought about children's circles (*circulos infantiles*), dining rooms in primary schools for the children of working mothers and scholarships for those who needed them, and it guaranteed work placements upon graduation from vocational, technical, professional and university programs. Families were provided with government-subsidized or free public healthcare services, including access to abortion and family planning. The Family Code included the specification that men were to share housework when women were gainfully employed. Women were guaranteed equal pay under the Constitution, and the Women's Commission on Employment operates to thwart discrimination in hiring and at the workplace.

These and other gender equality policy measures and actions instituted over the years were extended and reinforced in the wake of the U.N.'s New Millennium Goals. The gender dimension of these transformative changes, in terms of relations between women and men, and the improvement of conditions for women relative to men, are reflected in the following statistics. At the level of employment, the proportion of women in the labour force increased from 13 percent in 1959 to 39 percent in 1989. In the mid-1990s, the proportion of women in the labour force plateaued and then declined slightly, eventually recovering. In the latter half of the 1990s, it began to increase again. At present, more than 40 percent of the work force is composed of women, constituting an estimated 60 percent of the upper echelons of technicians and 67 percent of professionals. Women make up 61 percent of prosecutors, 49 percent of judges, 47 percent of magistrates and 30 percent of state administrators and ministry officials (Nuñez, 2007). Since 1978 women constitute over 50 percent of all professionals and technicians in the country and the female labour force is more educated than its male counterpart. By 2002, 48 percent of all economically active women had completed grade 12 and 10 percent were university educated, versus 37 percent and 11 percent of men, respectively. Women today constitute 60 percent of all university students and 47 percent of professors; 52 percent of scientists and medical doctors are women as are 70 percent of medical students and 50 percent of lawyers.

At the level of the labour market and employment, gender-equalizing policies and the resulting increased presence of women in the work force has had a positive impact on gender relations and identity throughout Cuban society. There was a dramatic decrease in discrimination in all senses. Nuñez emphasizes that Cuban women were the driving force behind these changes and the advances made. Cuban traditional macho culture remained a considerable cultural obstacle.

In education, Cuba has one of the highest rates of school enrolment of young girls in the world. Given that education is the major avenue of social empowerment in Cuba, the increased education of girls has led to their individual capacitation and realization of their human potential as contributors to Cuban society.

Progress has clearly been made by and for women in the Cuban Revolution as a result of public action taken from above and below. But these advances and improvements do not by any means signify that full gender equality has been achieved. For one thing, besides the persistence of sexist attitudes and male chauvinism, women are still under-represented in the higher echelons of power, particularly in the political sphere. However, Cuba performs well when compared to other countries. In terms of political representation of women, Cuba ranks first in the Americas (Lopez Vigil 1999:157). As to the participation of women in the National Assembly — Cuba's parliament — Cuba places tenth in the world. In recent years there has been a concerted effort to increase women's representation in the political, state and managerial structures and bodies, resulting, among other things, in an increased empowerment of women. The UNDP (2010) in this connection reports that while Cuba ranks fifty-first out of all countries on the HDI, it stands at twenty-ninth on its women's empowerment index.

In the 1998 national elections, the decline in the number of women representatives in the National Assembly that took place during the Special Period was reversed. Women's membership rose to 27.6 percent (August 1999:366). The 2003 elections saw women's parliamentary representation increase to 35.9 percent (Martinez Puentes, 2003:411), and, according to Save the Children's Mothers' Index (2010) as well as the UNDP (2010), 43 percent of government positions today are occupied by women. In the Council of State, the highest executive body, 16 percent of members are women. Saney notes that as he was writing his study of the Cuban Revolution in 2003, women headed five ministries: Science, Technology and the Environment; Interior Commerce; Finance and Prices; Foreign Cooperation and Investment; and Auditing and Control. Women also occupy 52.5 percent of union leadership positions and comprise more than 30 percent of the active membership of the Communist Party. In addition, women constitute 31 percent of all managers in state enterprises. Thus, despite the challenges of the Special Period and the succession of economic reforms that it helped to bring about, it is evident that the policies of the Cuban Revolution continue to embody "a clear willingness to achieve equality between men and women" (Lopez Vigil, 1999:173).

From a more critical perspective, sociological studies document the fact that Cuban women — like women elsewhere in both advanced and developing capitalist societies — also experience what has been called the double shift in the working day, dedicating on average up to thirty-six hours a week to domestic or household labour versus twelve hours for men (Nuñez, 2007). Because of the housing shortage, it is not unusual to find up to three generations of a family living under the same roof. Persistent patriarchal attitudes and a macho culture among men, which have survived all of the legislation thrown at them, ensure that women not only continue to assume responsibility for the bulk of domestic labour (*cocinar, limpiar, fregar y lavar*) but have the primary responsibility for social reproduction. The status of women is clearly a cultural artifact that has survived the transformation of a capitalist into a socialist society.

Conclusion

Equality, together with freedom and solidarity, is a fundamental value of socialist humanism. It is also the conceptual and ethical foundation of the Cuban Revolution and of socialist human development: development as equality, one might conclude, as opposed to development as freedom. In the UNDP conception of human development as freedom, equality appears not as a substantive social condition — that is, as an egalitarian society in which conditions are equal for all — but we find it as equity, an equality of opportunity, the essential condition of which is freedom rather than equality.

The difference is critical because capitalist societies are so structured as to render equality into an abstraction or a utopian ideal. Capitalism is fundamentally inegalitarian, characterized by a class hierarchy of relations and conditions. It cannot satisfy the system requirements for socialist human development at the level of equality or solidarity. Socialist human development on the other hand, grows from a deeply held egalitarianism which grows into a relatively egalitarian society in which conditions are equal for all. This is an equality that is not merely a matter of opportunity but a fundamental right and a necessary condition.

Cuba undoubtedly falls short as a fully egalitarian society, but there is no doubt that social equality is a vital element of the revolutionary consciousness that has been promoted by public action and national policy over the years. It has also been a fundamental organizing principle of the Revolution. One of the very first actions taken and policy measures adopted by the Revolutionary regime (in May 1960) was a radical land reform that reverted capitalism and reversed some of its abuses in the countryside; the conditions for 150,000 poor farmers were substantially improved. Over the course of the first two years relationships of production both in the countryside and in the urban centres were at first nationalized and then socialized. In this socialist process of productive transformation, the property of big landlords and capitalists, in both the agricultural and industrial sectors, were expropriated, but that of the small property holders were not. Unlike the Russian experience, smallhold farmers were not forcibly separated from their means of production, but were encouraged freely to combine their units of production into state farms or agricultural cooperatives. The nationalization and socialization process proceeded apace and was more or less completed by 1975, fifteen years into the Revolution, under conditions of free choice or voluntary submission.

The exception to this rule occurred in the Revolutionary Offensive of 1968, in which the service sector of small business operators was eradicated virtually overnight by administrative fiat. In this development both the market and the private sector were all but eliminated in a system of nationalized and socialized production. Only a small remnant of private enterprise remained in the agricultural sector. With the nationalization and socialization of production, the elimination of the labour market, with improved access to food and housing via public subsidies, and the socialization of public services in the sectors of health and education, Cuba completed the transition from capitalism to socialism, from a class-divided society characterized by relations and conditions of social inequality to a relatively egalitarian socialist society. The transition was not easy or free from mistakes and policy experiments, or shifts in economic strategy, but it was remarkably free from social conflict when compared to the experience of capitalist or social development elsewhere or previously.

6. Development as Freedom:
The Politics of Socialist Humanism

Socialism [in the twenty-first century] is the search for a fully
democratic society [based on] a culture that promotes...values such
as solidarity, humanism, respect for difference, and protection of the
environment and [that] turns its back on the view that hunger for
profit and the laws of the market are the guiding principles of human
activity.

— *Marta Harnecker (2010)*

It has been argued that, whereas the conceptual and ethical foundation of human
development within a capitalist system is the idea of freedom, socialism is founded
instead on the idea (and corresponding value) of equality, which requires more
substantive or system-transformative change for its realization. However, a careful
reading of the discourse of the Cuban Revolution — a discourse in which both
Fidel Castro and Che Guevara figure prominently — indicates that that freedom
is indeed a fundamental pillar of the Revolution. In Fidel's expression:

> Revolution is a sense of the historic moment; it is changing everything that
> should be changed; it is *complete equality and freedom*; it is being treated
> and treating others like human beings; it is *emancipating ourselves through
> ourselves*, and through our own efforts; it is defying powerful dominating
> forces inside and outside of the social and national sphere. (Fidel Castro,
> Speech, May 1, 2000)

Freedom in the context of the Cuban Revolution has an entirely different meaning
than it has for the ideologues and theorists of human development at the UNDP.
For the latter, freedom is understood (in social liberal terms) as an expansion of
choice and opportunities made available to individuals in order to realize their
human potential.[1] That is, the freedom is personal not collective. For the Cuban
revolutionaries freedom is understood in Marx's (1967a) socialist humanist
(rather than historical materialist) conception; it is understood as freedom from

want and exploitation, emancipation from relations and conditions of class rule and exploitation.

A close reading of Che Guevara's reflections suggest that this understanding of freedom is derived from a reading of Marx's socialist humanism in his early writings. For example, according to Marx, in class or class-divided societies, "personal freedom…exist[s] only for the individuals who *developed* under the conditions of the ruling class." But under the "real community" of communism (socialism), "individuals obtain their freedom in and through their association [with others]" (Marx, 1967b:87). Under socialism, instead of opportunities for individual development being obtained mainly at the expense of others, as in the competitive markets of class societies, the community provides "each individual [with] the means of cultivating his [or her] gifts in all directions; hence personal freedom becomes possible only within the community" (86, my emphasis). In short, communal property is individual insofar as it affirms each person's claim, as a member of society, for access to the productive resources, conditions and results of production as a conduit to her or his development as an individual "[for] whom the different social functions he performs are but so many modes of giving free scope to his own natural and acquired powers" (Marx, 1967a:488). Only in this way can "the old bourgeois society, with its classes and class antagonisms," be replaced with "an association in which the free development of each is a condition for the free development of all" (Marx & Engels, 1967b:53).

Within the overriding imperative of socialism — as Marx and Engels conceived of it — "the free development of individual human beings as social individuals" is embedded in an insistence that even within "the community of revolutionary proletarians … it is as individuals that people participate." And this is precisely because "it is the association of individuals … which puts the conditions of the free development and movement of individuals under their [own] control — conditions which were previously left to chance and that had acquired an independent existence over and against the separate individuals" (1967b:89). Stated differently, "the all-round realization of the individual will only cease to be conceived as an ideal … when the impact of the world that stimulates the real development of the abilities of the individual is under the control of the individuals themselves" (1967a:309), presumably by individuals as a collectivity or as a society.

Development as freedom

Cuba's achievement at the level of social development is beyond dispute. However, in the view of many scholars — although for many this view is filtered through an ideological lens — this achievement must be balanced against what is alleged to be a democratic deficit regarding the conception of development as freedom, that is, the freedom and the opportunity for individuals to choose and to act on their opportunities for self-realization and advancement, or the freedom to use their human abilities in order to allow them to live a life that they have reason to value.

The first of the UNDP's *Human Development Reports* (HDRs) in 1990 begins with the stirring words, "An irresistible wave of human freedom is sweeping across many lands. Not only political systems but economic structures are beginning to change in countries where democratic forces had been long suppressed." The Report continues, "People are beginning to take charge of their own destiny.... We are rediscovering the essential truth that people must be placed at the centre of development." The Report follows this rediscovery with the statement that the purpose of development is to "offer people more options," such as "access to income, a long life, knowledge, political freedom, personal security, community participation and guaranteed human rights." This turns out to be the UNDP's conception of development broadly defined as freedom: development understood as the expansion of choice and human abilities, or enlarging the range of people's choices.

Although the HDR defines freedom as the expansion of choice and the freedom to pursue the choices available to individuals, its architects and proponents have a decidedly non- or a-political conception of development. First, there is no political variable in the Human Development Index (HDI) used by the UNDP, in their comparative methods of ranking of countries to measure the level of human development achieved by each. The HDI does not measure in any way the politics of development, which is to say the "constraints on the opportunities available to the poor or the limits to their freedom." In this way, the UNDP does acknowledge the existence of such constraints, but it takes the developmental role of the state to be precisely the creation of a level playing field that eliminates barriers to choice and any restrictions on freedom. It further sees the role of the state as one that would introduce a policy of social exclusion and political reform in order to ensure that the inalienable rights of the individual (human rights) are respected and protected.

Even though the HDI itself does not include a method for measuring political freedom, human development as political freedom features significantly in a number of HDRs as a matter of principle and point of discussion. The central concern in this discussion is the degree to which human rights are respected and protected in practice. It is clear that the authors of these HDRs believe that human development can only flourish in conditions of economic and political "freedom" and that that economic freedom is understood as the right of individuals to pursue their personal interests, or for private-sector firms to seek a reasonable return on their investments and a profit on their operations. This is political freedom understood, in liberal democratic terms, as the rights of the individual. However, as we will argue below in regard to Cuba, freedom is no less an issue in a socialist context but understood very differently.

The profound value placed on freedom by the Cuban Revolutionary regime — and the fundamental meaning of the Revolution in terms of freedom as a condition of human development — was expressed eloquently and powerfully by Fidel Castro in the *First Declaration of Havana*, in his passionate denunciations of "Yanqui imperialism," of the obscene profits obtained by American corporations at the price of undernourishment and infant mortality in Latin America. To gauge the impact of Fidel's speech, and what it meant at the time not only for Cubans but for people across the region, it is useful to turn to a recent speech by Norman Girvan, a Jamaican economist and a member of the New World Group (founded by Lloyd Best), at his honorary doctorate acceptance speech at the University of Havana (December 3, 2008). In this speech, Girvan recounts the stirring words of Fidel Castro at the time, which were "still ringing in [his] ears" fifty years later. As he recounted his experience, "The image of a million Cubans, assembled in one place as the National General Assembly of the People of Cuba, expressing their approval of the social and economic measures taken by the Revolution, and declaring their independence of foreign domination, was a transformative experience.... It helped to shape [our] view of the world." Girvan elaborated on this point, "The Cuban Revolution was a source of inspiration to many of us [in] the ability of a small Caribbean country to chart its own course of social justice, economic transformation, and national independence by relying on the mobilization of the entire population, by relying on the will and energy of its people; with a leadership that trusted the mass of the population and refused to bow before threats, intimidation, economic punishment and counterrevolutionary violence from the greatest military power on the planet." He added, "It remains so to this day."

Based on the precept that popular participation is an essential condition of human development, practitioners at the UNDP and scholars in the liberal democratic tradition have argued that the Cuban model and the Revolution have been deficient in the following way: that decision-making is top-down, with power being held by an exceedingly small group in control of the state. The claim is that this provides few if any channels or institutional forms for popular participation. The hypothesis derived from this unsubstantiated theory (or ideology, as it may be seen) — which attributes extraordinary power to one individual (Fidel Castro), who is seen to dictate policy and events — is that the most important policy decisions are made by the Cuban government, with scant or no popular participation, and that a weak, if not entirely absent, civil society is subordinated to the state. At the same time, the argument goes, Cubans are denied all sorts of democratic or political freedoms, for example, the freedom freely to express their views and to organize and present the electorate with an alternative government program.

Notwithstanding the fact that the proponents of this widely held belief about Cuban politics tend to argue from an ideological standpoint with little to no empirical evidence, there are some grounds for arguing that Cuba suffers from a "democratic deficit." However, the evidence can be interpreted in various ways and suggest that the myth is based on the Cuban government's overreaction to an ongoing perceived (and not entirely fabricated) threat to national security. It is manifestly true that in the context of a true commitment to socialism as the systemic foundation of rational development, Cubans are in fact accorded all sorts of democratic freedoms. These freedoms are limited only by a fundamental respect for, and participation in, the revolutionary process. That is to say that within the Revolution everything is permitted, but outside of it, nothing is permitted. Although capitalist democracies seem to have a similar stricture regarding capitalism and democracy, the prejudice that ordinary Cubans do not participate in their own government is both arguable and continues to be highly contested.

From the standpoint that the defining characteristic and best protection of democracy is popular participation, the entire issue can be looked at somewhat differently. The issue becomes the institutional mechanisms and channels set up to promote and ensure participation. On this point there is a clear, although perhaps not fundamental, difference between human development as conceived and programed by the UNDP, and human development as institutionalized in the Cuban Revolution. For the UNDP (2003) participation is viewed (in terms established by Stiefel & Wolfe (1994), two economists at UNRISD and ECLAC) as a means of ensuring equality of opportunity and the participation of those hitherto excluded from any say in governance. In these terms the critical factor in the democratization process is to strengthen civil society: to ensure a vibrant and active counterweight to the state in the development process.

In Cuba popular participation is structured not so much on a strong vibrant civil society as it is in Local Bodies of People's Power (OLPP). These bodies are democratically elected representative parliaments whose purpose is formulation of public policy. Participation is also based on the mobilization of the entire population, which happened in response to the crisis of the 1990s. At that time, and since, there have been many examples of development initiatives within community-based organizations. Civil society organizations in Cuba are for the most part linked to the state in ways designed to ensure dialogue, cooperation and a two-way transmission of proposals, alternative ideas and initiatives.[2]

To take an example of how this has functioned in Cuba within this institutional set-up, Cubans, from all walks of life in their communities and workplaces, actively participated in designing the policy responses made by government to the worst production crises of the Special Period. Several scholars have argued that the mobilization of the population (some two million, it is estimated) in the form of workers' parliaments in 1993, to debate the issues and to search for a way out of the crisis, was a critical factor in producing the needed revolutionary consciousness (*la conciencia*). These parliaments are seen to have helped the Revolution survive the crisis: to hold the socialist line in a context of market reforms that threatened to undermine the pillars of the socialist human development model.

The politics of socialist development: People power and the state

Fidel Castro and Che Guevara declared that the Cuban Revolution was, fundamentally, a struggle for national liberation whose purpose was to liberate the country from imperialist exploitation and oppression. They saw the Revolution as a class struggle against exploitation and the oppressive oligarchical regime set up to enforce this exploitation. The revolution freed Cubans from a ruling minority that had been appropriating the lion's share of the social product and alienating most Cubans from their human essence (freedom and equality).

Together with other scholars (for example, Kirk & Erisman, 2009), the Cuban philosopher Miguel Limia (1999) argues that the struggle for freedom in Cuba — the struggle for liberation from the yoke of imperialist exploitation — should be traced back to the nineteenth-century Cuban struggle against American imperialism, and even earlier to the struggle for freedom from slavery and colonialism in the Spanish empire. According to Limia, the triumph of the revolutionary forces led to the implantation of a new social and political paradigm embedded in the writings and practice of José Martí, the revered mentor of the Cuban Revolution in regard to nationalism and anti-imperialism (Kirk 2012). Limia understood the new paradigm as a break with liberalism on key issues such as the nature of the human being, the nature of democracy and the need for a new consciousness and ethic regarding social justice. He also had differing views of pre-revolutionary (formally democratic) political systems. Above all, in Martí's interpretation, the Cuban Revolution represented a rupture with capitalism, the system that underlies the institutional framework of liberal democracy (hence the designation "capitalist democracy") and other elements of the ideological superstructure. Liberalism in this context can be understood as an orientation towards social and political reform, viewing change as progressive and liberating in the sense that it equalized opportunity for hitherto excluded groups and expanded choices available to individuals.

In this sense, the Cuban Revolution represented a rupture with capitalism as an economic system and liberalism as an ideology. Thus the Revolution can be seen as instituting what might be termed a socialist, as opposed to capitalist, democracy based on the participation of all citizens. This is not to say that the Cuban revolutionaries turned from liberalism to socialism as an explicit ideology (an idealized vision of another world and a better future) but rather, that they made this deliberate turn in order to mobilize action and mass support. The ideological underpinnings of the Cuban Revolution included nationalism — *la patria o muerte* — and human development. Socialism as an ideological framework for mobilizing action, and Marxism as theory, took immediate form in Cuba as humanism and active social participation. But another year of development in international relations passed before this took form as Marxism-Leninism. As Limia has it, "Marxism and Leninism would [come to] provide Cuban revolutionary thought with a new '*sustancia cosmovisiva*' [cosmo-vision] under historical conditions created by imperialist domination." He also recognizes that this driving philosophy sustains the continuing hostility of the United States to the Revolutionary regime.

According to Limia, the Provisional Revolutionary Government put into practice a socialist democracy, giving a voice to the people, guaranteeing popular participation in discussion and decision-making on issues of transcendental significance. "The key laws and political documents at the time," he argues, "were subject to intense and open debate and *aprobación populares*, or popular approval, and their implementation was left to the *surgidos del pueblo*, the new political actors formed at the grassroots."

Political power was achieved and defended by force, but Limia insists that it was "built with popular participation and a broad consensus as to the importance of common welfare and solidarity in a context of a class struggle for national sovereignty and social emancipation." More generally, he argues that revolutionary political power acquired its significance and deeper meaning because, for the first time this power was achieved and exercised in the name of the people, and for the first time, it was advanced to establish the sovereign right of Cuban people to decide for themselves and manage their own affairs, and to do so with a government of their own making. This "crucial historic fact," Limia argues, became a key feature and an essential element of a uniquely Cuban form of human development. It is clear when seen in this way that the Cuban Revolution is profoundly democratic and that participation is key to Cuba's democracy.

Having overthrown a bastion of the American empire in the hemisphere, the main political task in January 1959 was to construct "a unity of the people," converting diverse segments of the popular movement — "workers, peasants, intellectuals, students, youth...women" — into a "revolutionary mass surrounding the political vanguard of the Revolution." This task was carried out in order to construct a socialism based on *el desarrollo humano masivo* (massive popular participation). In the process of this revolutionary process, Cubans themselves "laid the foundation of a new state, a different type of civil society, and a new relationship between them (1999b)."

Institutional dynamics of national politics

In the wake of the 1968 Revolutionary Offensive, the Revolutionary leadership came to the conclusion that Cuban society could no longer operate on the basis of the existing institutional-policy framework. Consequently, there was a rethinking of the decision-making and policy formulation process and a search for a new institutional framework. In the early 1970s, Cuban political leaders announced their intention to begin what they called a "process of institutionalization" of the state and the political system.

While the 1960s had been the time of "taking heaven by storm," the 1970s were characterized by the institutionalization of the new economic, social and political order. The goal was to establish stable regulatory forms and the formal institutional setting for popular input in national decision-making. This included the passage of a new Cuban constitution and the reorganization of the political system, administrative structures and the legal system in order to create a structure more suited to the ideology and practice of a socialist political economy. This quest to institutionalize a Cuban form of participatory democracy also included a system of local government in the form of the "municipality, " which for José Martí was "the root...of freedom" and for Haroldo Dilla Alfonso (1993), a noted dissident and reactionary, "an experience beyond the paradigms. "

The institutionalization of the Revolution in 1976 was formally marked by the ratification of a new constitution in a popular referendum, by the establishment of the Local Bodies of People's Power — the first municipal system in revolutionary Cuba — and the establishment of the Municipal and National Assemblies of People's Power.

Debating democracy in Cuba

Beyond Elections: Redefining Democracy in the Americas is an important documentary film that explores the vital question, "What is Democracy?" (Fox & Laindecker, 2008). In its search for an answer the film takes us on a journey across the hemisphere from Venezuela's communal councils to Brazil's participatory budgeting process, from the emergence of constitutional assemblies within the indigenous communities of Bolivia to the formation of grassroots movements in the region, from the "recovery" by Argentinean workers of their factories to the construction of cooperatives and alternative forms of economic production and social organization.

A democratic wind, the filmmaker suggested, was blowing across Latin America at the turn of the millennium, in the form of an experimentation with new forms of popular participation that were going well beyond the electoral process of voting. Within the liberal democratic system, democracy is defined formally in terms of the "rule of law," on the basis of the political party apparatus and use of the electoral mechanism to secure a system of representation and participation in making decisions and public policy. However, as the film makes clear — and the UNDP has long argued — democracy is much more than elections. It is "a long-term process of reorganizing the institutions of civil society.... [the participation of people] in events and process that shape their lives" (UNDP, 1993: iii).

As for political democracy, Cuba has demonstrated that the institution of multi-party politics and direct elections is not the only way of organizing democracy. Workplace and community councils can produce an alternate system that is representative and participatory, and thus arguably democratic.[3] As for the form that democracy is theorized to take at the level of respect for human rights and free elections, numerous political analysts — notably including Eduardo Galeano, Amy Goodman, Emir Sader, Martha Harnecker, Ward Churchill and Leonardo Avritzer — have noted the emergence in Latin America of experimentation with different and new forms of participation and democracy. These exercises in democracy have ranged from Cuba's Local Bodies of People's Power (OLPPS) and People's Councils, and participatory budgeting in Brazil, to the formation, in Venezuela, of tens of thousands of self-organized Communal Councils in an experiment in local self-government or decentralized democratic governance.[4]

Around the world, by the UNDP's reckoning, 120 countries now have at least the minimum trappings of democracy, the freedom to vote for all citizens (with only a few exclusions). For many in the global south however, this is just the beginning, not the end. Following decades of U.S.-engineered or -backed dictatorships, civil wars and devastating structural adjustment policies in the south, and also imperialism and corporate control, electoral corruption and fraud, representative politics in the Americas is in serious crisis. People are choosing to redefine democracy in their own terms: local, direct and participatory: socialist. In 1989, the Brazilian Workers' Party altered the concept of local government when they installed participatory budgeting in Porto Alegre, allowing residents to participate directly in the allocation of city funds. Ten years later, Hugo Chávez swept into power with the promise of granting direct participation to the Venezuelan people. As it turned out, diverse forms of popular participation, especially in the form of Communal Councils, were subsequently established, both as an initiative "from above" and spontaneously "from below." In Argentina, a growing number of factories have been "recovered" from their owners by the workers, and across Latin America social movements and popular assemblies have taken form, taking power away from the dominant class and the ruling elites and putting it directly into the hands of their members and citizens.

The debate continues but it is evident that these direct and local forms of citizen participation have produced a more substantive form of democracy than that which prevails in the capitalist democracies of the "West." They have incorporated the hitherto excluded poor majority in decision-making processes. These experiments have also thrown light on the democratic nature of the system devised in Cuba for public action and citizen participation.

Arnold August (1999) argues that the Cuban approach to democracy has produced a system that is more representative than is the case in capitalist democracies. Cuba's system is based on the guaranteed rights and the opportunity and freedom of all citizens to participate in the electoral process without the constraints (lack of money, for example) that surround elections in capitalist democracies. The relative absence of such constraints on political participation in Cuba is reflected in the dynamics of political representation in the electoral process. In liberal democracies such as the U.S. and Canada, there is a notable divergence between the social classes or groups that achieve political power by electoral means and the distribution of these groups in society as a whole. In these systems there is a virtual absence of any direct representation of the common worker, housewife, family farmer or other more menial worker. In Cuba, however, it is quite different. There is no such divergence between the social class of those holding power and the distribution of these classes in the general population. The Cuban electoral system, in which the one party (which is to say, the PCC) is not allowed to participate in the process, results in a system that is arguably democratic in terms of the right and the freedom of all citizens to participate actively, as well as in terms of the principles of representation and accountability.

In spite of the UNDP's perennial concern with the "density of the state" in Cuba, and in spite of the perception of a Cuban "democratic deficit" on the part of so many non-Cuban liberal (or bourgeois) political scientists, Cuba's approach has resulted in a democratic system, in a socialist democracy in which citizens are free to participate actively, within the limits of respect for the system and the revolutionary process, that is, respect for the institution of the Cuban state. This of course is a basic principle of any democracy: that freedom does not extend to the right, and active efforts, to subvert the system or betray the people. But democracy, whether capitalist or socialist, should mean maximum freedom within these limits. As Marta Harnecker emphasized in a recent interview, "socialism is the search for a *fully* democratic society."

But this debate continues, and it could be argued that the security concerns of the Cuban state result in undue restrictions on basic democratic rights: the rights to freely express opinions and to organize. In this connection, some scholars and Cuban dissidents (see Dilla Alfonso, 1993, for example) argue that Cuba suffers from a "democratic deficit": or they use security concerns to stifle dissent. But arguments along these lines are usually advanced without any scientific evidence and are saturated with ideological bias. It could be argued that under conditions that prevail in most capitalist democracies, the freedom to participate meaningfully in the political process is severely constrained. It could also be argued that the freedom of expression that does exist does not have much political power if, as is usually the case, the means of mass communication are in the hands of a powerful elite and there are few meaningful opportunities to express dissent regarding the existing economic system. Although the mechanisms for manufacturing consent and stifling dissent in capitalist democracies are different, and perhaps less obvious and public, they are nonetheless at least as effective. Just as is the case in Cuba, when someone in a capitalist country transgresses the limits of dissent (subversion or betrayal of the system of government) he or she is held in line, if not imprisoned or worse.

Even so, the apparent intolerance of Cuban officials — particularly that of PCC members, whose self-assigned role is to ensure respect for the socialist system and the revolutionary process, and to be on the watch for counterrevolutionaries — remains an issue of concern. It is claimed that, notwithstanding its human development achievements, Cuba is far from being a "fully democratic society." Indeed, as argued by the economist Esteban Morales (a member of the Unión de Escritores y Artistas de Cuba [Union of Writers and Artists of Cuba, or UNEAC]) and who was separated from the PCC for public statements about official corruption), "corruption is the true counterrevolution" and is "much more dangerous than the internal dissent that led to the 2003 crackdown" (Morales, 2010).

Cuba's leadership, it should be pointed out, has acknowledged that the government and the PCC had made a serious error in placing too many restrictions on "intellectual liberty." For instance, in January 2007, the Minister of Culture Abel Prieto told the writers' association that during the 1970s, hardliners in the regime conducted witch hunts, especially against homosexual intellectuals but also against artists and intellectuals too attuned to a worldview hostile to socialism and the Revolution. Many received apologies and several people who were once censored are now in leading positions. Some, such as Antón Arrufat and Miguel Barnet, have been awarded the national prize for literature. Nevertheless, it could be argued that the Cuban Revolution is still opposed to some types of dissent.

The Comités de Defensa de la Revolución (CDRs): Security versus freedom
In the liberal democratic tradition of political thought of John Locke and others, freedom is counterposed to security, and the state is viewed as a necessary evil, with which members of society express their willingness to sacrifice some degree of freedom in exchange for security. It is this pay-off and a presumed willing submission of citizens to the laws of the state that explain Jacques Rousseau's critique of liberal democracy's social contract: "Man is born free but everywhere he is in chains."

A similar counterpoint between freedom and security, it could be argued, can be found in the workings of the Cuban CDRs (Committees for the Defence of the Revolution); these are a network of community-based organizations across the island, with an estimated membership of over 7.6 million. But the security exchanged in the process is social rather than political in form. That is, just as the economic freedom of the individual is limited by the superior claims of equality and solidarity, the political rights and freedom of the individual is subordinated, within limits, to the security of the population as a whole and the freedom of *la patria*, the country.

The CDR system was formed on September 28, 1960, as "a collective system of revolutionary vigilance," to report on: "Who lives on every block? What does each do? What relationship does each have with tyrants? To what is each dedicated? In what activities is each involved? And, with whom does each meet?"[5] Set up as an organization designed to protect the Revolution — to prevent counterrevolutionaries from acting like termites to undermine the Revolution from within — the CDR has been the subject of considerable criticism and endless debate. From a liberal democratic perspective they are naturally viewed as neighbourhood watch organizations formed to spy on neighbours, constituting not only a home security organization but also a non-democratic means of silencing dissent and policing as well as monitoring behaviour. Needless to say, the Revolutionary leadership sees the CDRs in a different light: instead, they think of them as essential organizations for domestic and national security. They are meant to protect the hard-fought freedoms won by the Revolution.

Since the CDRs system was set up, it has raised questions about the committees' functional dynamics: whether or not and how they have changed over time as the presumed threat to internal and national security abated. Curiously, there have been very few social scientific studies into the functioning of CDRs. Those that have been published invariably reflect the ideological bent of the studies' authors. Foreign, mostly American, scholars tend to view the CDRs as a fundamental threat to essential freedoms, as restricting the capacity of Cubans from expressing their views and from organizing freely. While it is understood that the CDRs act ostensibly in the name of fighting counterterrorist activity, they are seen by most studies to function as the dreaded STASI (the Ministry for State Security) of the German Democratic Republic.

On the other hand, proponents of the CDRs and many Cuban scholars tend to stress the important role played by CDRs not only in stabilizing home security (for help during times of natural disasters) but in promoting social and community-based local development projects, and organizing mass rallies in support of the revolutionary process. Proponents also emphasize that CDRs put medical, education and other campaigns into national effect and that, being organized on a geographical basis, they also act as centres for many who do not work in farms or factories. For example, they include a large proportion of female membership (Thomas, 1971:996).

Regarding the centrality to Cuban society of community-based neighbourhood organizations such as the CDRs, there has surged a debate over whether Cuba can be thought to have a civil society or whether such organizations are merely conduits for the government line on public policy and its view of proper thinking and behaviour (Marín-Dogan, 2008).

Civil society, the state and democratic politics

The functioning of the CDRs and their role in the revolutionary process have raised the question of whether the *barrio* CDRs constitute a mechanism of government control over the population that ensures people toe the line or, on the contrary, whether they serve as a locus of civil social organization, or as mechanisms of social democracy or popular participation in public action. From the former perspective, critics have noted that it was the local CDR of the PCC in the Havana municipality of Playa that forced the expulsion of Esteban Morales (mentioned earlier in the chapter) to silence a voice that was raised not in dissent from the government line or the system, but as part of an internal debate on the nature and future of Cuban socialism, a debate that by any democratic account should be open and free. It must be kept in mind that CDRs are by no means the only community or *barrio*-based expression of people's power in Cuba, nor the only organizational expression of Cuba's vibrant civil society.

Research reviewed in Alexander Gray's and Antoni Kapcia's 2008 book on Cuban civil society points to the growing importance of the *barrio* CDRs as the locus of a civil society, organizing to promote and advance local development. The municipal, provincial and national Asambleas del Poder Popular (Assemblies of People's Power, or APP) were constituted in 1976 to provide real, regular and more systemic and systematic forms through which people could participate in running the society. The exercise of social and political democracy through elective state bodies is a principle of socialist development, though in Cuba its implementation was delayed after the triumph of 1959 (García Brigos, 2001:13).

The APPs constitute a distinctly Cuban form of democratic participation in the affairs of the country and decision-making at all levels of political organization. They were designed to function as an institutional form of social and political democracy, understood as self-government. In 1986, the institutional form of people's power was modified and became the Consejos Populares (People's Councils), the embryo for what was regarded as a superior form of self-government and democracy. Growing disillusion with the system of popular power led to reforms in democratic governance, beginning in Havana in 1989. The Nuevos Consejos Populares (New People's Councils), with full-time administrators to tend to local concerns, were introduced and in 1992 opened throughout the country. The revised Constitution of 1992 granted the electorate the right to elect Provincial Assembly representatives and National Assembly representatives directly. Municipal representatives had been elected directly since 1976. Incorporated into the 1992 Constitution as part of the state system, the People's Councils supplemented, rather than supplanted the OLPP as a means of providing a more active approach to democratic political participation. The aims were to engage ordinary citizens more fully in the affairs of state and to strengthen popular participation. The People's Councils also created a broader group of social actors to coordinate the tasks of government. As such, they were linked to both the OLPP and *organizaciones de masas,* or mass organizations, such as the Communist Party and the Federation of Cuban Women, which, in the view of some are merely adjuncts of the state apparatus, while others see them as an expression of civil society.

Civil society and the state

The notion of civil society as an amalgam of social organizations formed outside the state system is a concept of the eighteenth-century Enlightenment, resurrected in the 1980s in a context of a movement to democratize capitalist development and the state, to engage civil society in taking responsibility for development and for ensuring governability and good governance (Bardhan, 1997; OECD, 1997; UNDP, 1993; World Bank, 1994). Until the eighties in fact, capitalist development had been notoriously undemocratic, with key decisions made by small elites that controlled the institutions of economic and political power. National politics was nominally democratic in the sense that power-holders were subjected to periodic democratic elections. It can be clearly observed, however, that the power of the democratic vote, as a means of allowing the people to determine policy, cannot match the power of money.

In this context it was argued that the only way to secure a substantive democracy, or a more than nominal participation, was to strengthen civil society: to create an alternative organizational base to encourage popular contribution to public decision-making. And indeed this has been the history of democracy in Latin America since the mid-1980s; it has been a struggle to strengthen and engage civil society in the process of public policy formation.

As noted above, the institutional basis for this process was a policy of decentralization that was mandated and widely implemented as the price of admission into the "new world order." The aim of the policy was to create the institutional framework for "good governance," a more participatory and inclusive form of local development with the agency of community-based forms of organization and the strategic support of a civil society (Mitlin, 1998).

In the 1990s the push towards "democratization" and "democratic development" was no longer expressed primarily in terms of a concern for establishing the rule of law and increasing participation in electoral politics. Instead, democratization came to mean the strengthening of civil society — that is, nongovernmental organizations — relative to the state, and to mean ensuring the accountability of politicians and state officials to the people. In the context of the growing global "people's power" and pro-democracy movements, the understanding held by mainstream social and political scientists regarding the relationship between development and democracy changed radically. Hitherto it had been argued by many that what was needed for development were strong leaders and authoritarian governments. Democracy was seen as messy, more often than not leading to political instability and social conflict rather than economic growth. But it was increasingly argued that the best way to promote development was through a strong civil society.

This shift in thinking about development and democracy also changed the debates about and in Cuba. Hitherto the focus of the debate of Cuba's civil society on the part of American and other analysts had been on the institutional structure of the electoral process, specifically on the absence of political parties in Cuba, and on the importance of the role they play in liberal democracies. In the 1990s, however, in the wake of this renewed interest in civil society and in decentralizing governmental decision-making on development, the question became whether Cuba had a civil society which could counter the weight of the state and allow for popular participation in decision- and public policy-making.

As has been stated before, answers to this question have been given by and large with weighted ideological bias, rather than on the basis of empirical research and scientific analysis. Many American and European social scientists (for example, Dilla Alfonso & Oxhorn, 2002) continue to view Cuban mass organizations as part of the state, without considering their capacity to exert a countervailing force on state officials, or to oppose the powerful interests that have such an influence in capitalist democracies. However, a number of scholars, both Cuban and non-Cuban, have entered the fray to argue the contrary. Arnold August (2013) and Isaac Saney (2003) are good examples.[6]

Democracy as electoral politics and popular participation

Democracy, like freedom, takes different forms but it is usually defined by scholars from capitalist countries in terms of the principles of political representation, participation in public policy formation, and the institutional expressions of these principles. In the liberal tradition of representative democracy and electoral politics, political representation is often merely the business of elites while participation is commonly reduced to the periodic electoral mobilization of isolated voters. It could also be argued that the distinctive feature of representative democracy is not the holding of elections as such but an institutional setting that allows citizens to influence the dynamics of representative institutions on a continuous and regular basis. In these terms the critical democratic issue is the nature of the relationship between the state and civil society, or, more precisely, the mediating structures that facilitate the participation of civil society actors in the public policy arena.

As a means of understanding the distinct forms taken by civil society and participation, Selee and Peruzzotti (2009) have identified three main approaches, each of which advances a different model for analysis: 1. social capital model; 2. public sphere model; and 3. pressure-group politics model. Each approach focuses on specific types of participation involving specific actors. To account for the diversity of civic initiatives that generally form civil society, Selee and Peruzzotti argue that these approaches need to be brought together.

As for Cuba, analysis of the civil society–state relationship and of the dynamics of popular participation in public policy has generally been shaped by a combination of analyses of the public sphere and social capital models. In terms of the former, emphasis is placed on the construction, early on in the revolutionary process, of civic organizations in the workplace and the community linked to the state so as to allow for a two-way flow of information and policy inputs. Examples of such organization would be the CDRs, the FMC and the UNEAC.

Mainstream scholars in the liberal bourgeois tradition of political science cast aspersions on these and other such organizations, which they generally regard as government set-ups. From this perspective the institutional channels and mediating structures between state and civil society in Cuba are seen merely as conduits of government control, that is, to pass down the government line on public policy. However, several studies (see Saney, 2003; August, 2013) suggest that these organizations are legitimate functional expressions of an effective, if limited, civil society, and that the link they provide to the state constitutes a two-way channel which allows neighbourhoods and workers to receive and debate the government line on public policy and then to participate actively in policy-making by voicing their opinions to local leadership.

In liberal democratic discourse, participation has different meanings, ranging from participation of citizens in periodic elections to the active discussion in workplaces and neighbourhoods of public policy options available to their elected representatives. The associated dynamics often are analyzed from an ideological as well as a theoretical standpoint. In the case of Cuba a number of studies in recent years have challenged the opinions, widely held among American, Canadian and European political scientists, that democracy in Cuba is a sham; that decisions are made at the top, in fact by a single leader (Fidel and then Raúl); and that the participation of civil society in the public policy process is limited to rubber stamping decisions that are made at the top.

Conclusion

Appearances, as Marx observed, are often deceiving, contradicting the underlying reality. This is the case for Cuba, which has the appearance of a somewhat authoritarian welfare or socialist state, with decisions made at the top. But in reality, there are multiple means for the active participation of ordinary Cubans from all walks of life in public policy and the development process.

This feature of the Cuban model of socialist development in fact explains many outcomes: how the Revolution managed to survive the crisis precipitated by the collapse of the socialist bloc; how it retained essential and broad support for the revolutionary process under conditions of continuing hardship and austerity. Participation at every level of society also explains Cuba's continuing achievements in human development; these would not have been possible were it not for the effective institution of revolutionary consciousness through active participation in an ongoing revolutionary process.

7. Agricultural Change and Sustainable Development

Capitalism has generally advanced over the years on the basis of agriculture — and, not to put too fine a point on it — by dispossessing the direct small landholding agricultural producers (family farmers) of their land and means of production This process has resulted in their impoverishment, forced out-migration and proletarianization,[1] and the exploitation of the unlimited supplies of surplus labour generated by the capitalist development of agriculture. The process of productive and social transformation that has accompanied the capitalist "development" of the forces of production in the Americas also led to the displacement and sometimes to the complete destruction of entire native populations as well as a long-term and rather dramatic movement of populations from the rural communities to the towns and cities. These demographic changes demonstrated what Marx saw as a fundamental contradiction of capitalism, namely, the relationship between town and country, which itself parallels the capital-labour relationship in that both are based on exploitation.[2]

As the process of urbanization proceeds parallel to industrialization, modernization and capitalist development of economies and societies, the contradiction between country and town (reflected in increased social inequalities) becomes sharper and sharper as the population is pushed or pulled into the growing metropolis. In 1950 only one-third of the world's population was classified as urban. Fifty years on, at the end of the century, after more than four decades of capitalist development, over 72 percent lived in cities. This bare fact signals one of the most dramatic demographic shifts in all of human history, and is paralleled by equally massive international migration, most of it labour-based.

These processes of large-scale and rapid urbanization and of social transformation that have marked the paths of transition towards capitalism have been called "the agrarian question" (Bernstein, 2012). Stages in the course of this agrarian transformation include the following:

- dispossession of direct agricultural producers (small landholding family farmers) by diverse means, often by force involving violent expropriation, but also by enclosure of common land and the dynamic forces of capitalist development;

- forced abandonment of agriculture as a source of livelihood by these smallhold family farmers;
- the concentration of land and capital into fewer and fewer hands, resulting in a condition of landlessness or near-landlessness of a large and growing part of the rural population;
- capitalist development of agriculture based on the transformation of rich farmers into commercial farmers and capitalist entrepreneurs;
- the eradication of pre-capitalist relationships of agricultural production and the expansion of the capitalist nucleus in the urban centres;
- wholesale large-scale demographic shifts of the rural population into these modern urban centres and mega-cities, with a large part of this population absorbed by the burgeoning "informal sector" and the associated "planet of slums"[3]; and
- the transformation of small-scale and biodiverse local production intended for local food markets into production of commercial crops and, as a consequence, the loss not only of biodiversity, but food security and food sovereignty, as small-scale producers struggle to resist and survive the powerful forces of capitalist development.

When conceptualized in terms of these dynamic processes the agrarian question can be seen as a general movement towards capitalism. However, the agrarian question can also apply to socialist development or the path taken by some countries towards socialism. And what about the socialist development of agriculture? The celebrated cases of Russia and China are telling and disturbing, pointing as they do to an inhuman process of forced collectivization, a use of systemic and political violence that paralleled the harsh and brutal consequences of the capitalist development processes. Indeed, some argue that in the case of Russia and China the productive and social transitions towards socialism were much worse than they were in capitalism, in that they led not only to the eviction and forced abandonment of agriculture and the rural population's livelihood and rural communities, but in mass starvation, by some accounts, of tens of millions of smallhold farmers.

Where and how does this apply to the Cuban Revolution? What form did the social organization of agriculture assume, and under what conditions has it evolved over time? With regard to the socialist development of agriculture, this chapter argues that certain unique developments in the history of the Cuban Revolution led it to diverge in crucial ways from the agrarian and agricultural experiences of other nations that attempted socialist revolutions in the twentieth century. The form taken by socialist agriculture in Cuba has been better suited to achieving goals of human development and ecological sustainability than earlier models, either capitalist or socialist.

Cuba has in fact pioneered an approach to agrarian change and agricultural development that provides important lessons for other countries in the search for a model that is both ecologically sustainable and capable of overcoming the contradictions of capitalist development. This approach resolved problems that in different parts of the world have reached crisis proportions: rural poverty and food insecurity, what has been called the "metabolic rift" in agriculture,[4] and the unsustainability of rural livelihoods, cooperative forms of organization and small-scale production for local markets.

The transformation of Cuban agriculture

At the time of the Revolution the rural population represented around 56 percent of the population, most of it engaged directly or indirectly in agriculture, working the land as small-scale and small landowning farmers or as tenant farmers. Today, after several decades of heavy and steady rural-urban migration, 74 percent of Cuba's eleven million people live in urban areas: a little over the average for countries in the region. However, unlike the situation in most other Latin American countries, a not insignificant part of the rural population had already been proletarianized as cane workers, working for miserable wages harvesting sugar in the cane fields. Sugar already constituted Cuba's largest export by volume and value. In fact, some sociologists attribute the successes of the Revolution to the fact that an oppressed and exploited rural proletariat is more likely to form a class consciousness of their situation, which is to say, an awareness of their exploitation by a largely absentee class of agrarian, commercial and industrial capitalists. This consciousness meant that they were more easily converted to socialism and the socialization of agricultural production. In fact, the main social base of the Cuban Revolution was made up of both smallhold farmers and rural populations appropriated as wage-labourers.

Land reform and the collectivization process

Shortly after taking state power, the new Revolutionary government in Cuba initiated a process of agrarian reform that, while initially rather modest, rapidly escalated and dramatically transformed agricultural production and the social conditions of the rural population. One of the first decrees of the new administration on achieving state power, the Agrarian Reform Law of 1959, was to redistribute the land to farmers. Similar land reforms were subsequently instituted all over Latin America as a measure designed to dampen revolutionary ferment and the demand for radical change in the countryside. However, none of these land reforms were as far-reaching as Cuba's.

The first round of land appropriation targeted the colonial sugar cane *latifundia* and the massive tracts of pasture owned by a small and wealthy landlord elite. The Instituto Nacional de Reforma Agraria (National Institute for Agrarian Reform, or INRA),[5] expropriated around six million hectares of farmland (four million of which were either sugar plantations or pasture) and made Cuba's 123,000 smallhold farmers the owners of their land, redistributing some 400,000 hectares to small producers. With the second Agrarian Reform law, enacted in 1963, the state expropriated over 70 percent of the nation's farmland, while the remainder of private lands were turned over in title to smallhold farmers (Nova, 2002:29). Most of the land expropriated was placed under state ownership and in the years following the reforms consolidated into massive state farms. By the end of the agrarian reform process in the latter part of the 1960s both pre-capitalist and capitalist social relations in land and agriculture had been all but extinguished. They were supplanted by a system of planned socialist agriculture and land use. Most of the farms outside the sugar sector were also collectivized, in the form of cooperatives and state farms.

The first Agrarian Reform law, enacted in May 1959, entailed the confiscation of the property and assets embezzled by officials of the overthrown Batista regime; the expropriation of rental housing for social distribution (housing rents were reduced by 50 percent); state intervention in economic enterprises (factories, warehouses, transportation) that had been abandoned by their owners or in which labour conflicts disrupted production; and the confiscation of property of those who had failed to pay taxes or were either convicted of counterrevolutionary crimes or in exile.

As for the land reform, most of the *latifundia*, particularly the sugarcane plantations and cattle ranches, were taken over and the land redistributed either among farm labourers, who had worked it without ownership, or they were converted into state-run agricultural enterprises or cooperatives, thereby initiating what was indeed an agrarian revolution, not just a reform.

In the second half of 1959 and into the 1960s the scope and scale of the socialization process increased and was extended to all U.S.- or foreign-owned oil refineries, U.S.-owned sugar mills, banks, businesses and utilities. In March 1959 the Revolutionary government nationalized the Cuban Telephone Company. The Ministry for the Recovery of Embezzled Goods nationalized fourteen sugar mills and in April 1959 announced that it had recovered more than US$400 million for the people. On June twenty-ninth, in response to U.S. aggression, the ministry took over Texaco and on July first, ESSO and Shell. And in August, all U.S. companies in the oil, communications and electricity sectors were nationalized. In October, this nationalization process, a form of socialization in the name and cause of national liberation (arguably a socialist condition of human development), was extended to all domestic and foreign banks and large capitalist enterprises, including 105 sugar mills, fifty textile companies and eight railroad companies. By the end of the first decade all domestic wholesale and foreign trade and banking, most transportation, industry, construction and retail trade, and more than one third of agriculture were under state ownership and control.

This transfer of ownership effectively liquidated capitalism and severely restricted the workings of the non-capitalist market. Several government agencies were created to regulate what remained of private economic activity and to substitute central planning for the market. The Central Planning Board (JUCEPLAN) was initially established in March 1960 not as an agency for central planning, but to coordinate government policies and to guide the private sector through indicative planning, much as occurred in Japan and emerging Asian newly industrialized countries. Financing of economic development was also coordinated and conducted through the state by the Ministry of Finance and the National Bank, with private financing restricted to agriculture. The Ministry of Labour, according to Mesa-Lago — who, like most bourgeois liberals and other well-known Cuban dissidents, is averse if not hostile to socialism in any form — played an important role in establishing labour conditions. As Mesa-Lago put it, this was "the first step toward taming trade unions" (2000:177).

The socialization process provoked the exodus not only of the ruling class of owners but of a wide swath of managers, technicians and professionals of all sorts. In sociological terms, these were the professional-managerial or upper middle class. However, the Revolutionary government acted swiftly to replace this class through an extensive and open professional training and education program. This effected a policy that would take some years to iron out but that ultimately would bear fruit in the formation of a new cadre of professionals who were solidly committed to the revolutionary project.

As for economic development, the leadership saw the island's problems to be due to Cuba's sugar monoculture and dependence on export revenue. The first strategy in dealing with this problem was to lessen the dependence and diversify economic production by means of an import substitution strategy.[6] The leadership also initiated a program of agricultural diversification. Another aspect of the leadership's economic strategy, undertaken between 1960 and 1963, was a move to reduce dependence on the U.S., a move that included signing a trade agreement with the U.S.S.R. This agreement committed the Soviet Union to buying one million tonnes of sugar annually. In return they were to supply oil, machinery and chemicals. In the mid-sixties U.S.-owned refineries refused to refine Soviet crude. As a result, they were nationalized; by the end of the year practically all of Cuba's oil was imported from the Soviet Union. In retrospect, this can be seen as the new economic dependency that it was; it would spell near disaster twenty-five years later with the collapse of the U.S.S.R. and its trade relationship with Cuba.

At the level of labour, the hitherto dominant capital-labour relationship had been broken. In 1960, the government (that is, the Ministry of labour) began to set wages and regulate labour conditions. From a human development perspective this was an important change, since the government by means of a pay-scale mechanism was able in short order to ensure a relatively equitable social distribution of national income; by the end of the 1960s most of this distribution took the form of wages for work. Because of the socialization of labour that took place at this time — or "collectivization" as Mesa-Lago would have it — employment in the state sector grew from 9 percent to about one half of the labour force (Mesa-Lago, 2000:178).

In the agricultural sector, the island's seasonal employment was reduced not so much by public action as by structural change and by the result of the decisions on the part of thousands of rural workers to migrate to the cities, especially Havana. In this process the population of Havana in the 1960s increased at a rate that was twice what it had been in the 1950s. The children of these migrant families were given immediate and equal access to a growing number of schools, constructed as a matter of priority, while the migrants themselves were largely absorbed into the rapidly growing labour market for armed forces jobs, those in state security and police, unions and other popular organizations, and for employment in public works and social services. In addition, thousands of young rural workers received scholarships for education programs. While these programs delayed their entry into the labour market, the education facilitated a process of social transformation that changed smallhold farmers and rural workers into an urban working and middle class.

A key aspect of this process was a massive literacy campaign conducted by thousands of volunteer teachers that virtually eliminated illiteracy in less than a year and dramatically improved the social condition of the rural poor. From a human development perspective this period had a transcendental significance. In other parts of Latin America the same process of productive and social transformation (modernization, urbanization and capitalist development) was well underway, but outside Cuba, this process was subject to the vicissitudes and painful adjustments of the market. In these countries, this led to the absorption of rural surplus labour, not into work for wages but into "work on one's account" in the burgeoning informal sector and associated "planets of slums" (Davis, 2006).[7] The rural-to-urban migrants in other countries of Latin America at this time were generally excluded from public education; this is reflected in significantly higher rates of illiteracy and lower levels of human development there compared with those of Cuba.

In spite of the relatively low level of labour remuneration and the scepticism of economists in the liberal tradition, the vast majority of Cuba's former rural workers were decidedly better off as a result of the new labour regime. For one thing, the government provided each family with a minimum ration of basic goods, which reduced the dependence of rural households on earned income to meet their basic needs. Except for agriculture, collectivization virtually eliminated dividends, rents and interest forms of income. The rate of unemployment was also reduced and a relatively flat pay-scale in the state sector ensured an unprecedented degree of equity or fairness in the social distribution of income.

This, of course, is another measure of human development. No longer would a small upper and middle class of well-to-do individuals be able to appropriate and dispose of the lion's share of the social product, leaving the bulk of the population to fend for itself in the interstices or on the margins of the system. To the degree that meeting the basic needs of the entire population and improving the standards of living with an appreciable degree of equity are fundamental principles of socialist human development, the Cuban Revolution delivered quickly and early on the promise of a more human form of society, albeit under difficult economic conditions with a very sporadic rate of economic growth. Under these conditions aggregate income actually expanded as a result of the extension of free education and healthcare and subsidized housing, as well as the reduction of electricity rates and urban housing rates by as much as 50 percent.

Mesa-Lago (2000) makes passing reference to the humanity of this development, but in his concern about the alleged "Stalinist command system" of centralized planning, he neglects its social and political significance for human development. The concentration of fiscal expenditures on expanding social services in the rural areas in Cuba at this time reduced the urban-rural gap in living standards and ensured a very high level of support for the Revolution in those areas. This is a political development that most clearly distinguishes the Cuban Revolution from the Russian. Ernest Mandel notes, "the Cuban Revolution is distinguished by the fact that it succeeded in both gaining and maintaining the support of most of the popular masses for the revolutionary project" (1967). It is also distinguished from the Russian Revolution in its profound commitment to a socialist ethic of human development, a commitment evidenced in the continuing active engagement of both the leadership and the population in the revolutionary process.

The agriculture-industry contradiction and social conditions of rural socialist development

The rural population of Cuba made substantial social gains in the decades that followed the Revolution. The Revolution approached the countryside with a massive program of investment in the health, education, and general social well-being of the working classes. The advancements in general education and into university-level and technical training, enabled the Cuban rural working populace to transition, in the space of a generation, from a generally malnourished, illiterate, heavily exploited and oppressed population into what is one of the best educated and well trained agrarian labour forces in Latin America. Cuba is the only country in the region, if not the world, where the social condition of the rural working population is on average better than that of the urban working population. One indication of this is the fact that the remuneration of agricultural labour in Cuba today is higher than that of intellectual workers and highly educated urban professionals in the field of medicine. Cuba has made available to its agricultural labour force a full array of public services, and there is a conspicuous absence of exploitative social relations or physically and mentally degrading labour processes. A statistic telling of this concern for rural social development is the difference in life expectancy of sugar workers in Brazil and Cuba: some thirty years, according to one study.

The transformation of Cuba's agriculture from its former state of exploitation and oppression into a modern industrial system with vastly improved social conditions could only have been accomplished with a collective labour power of large sectors of the Cuban population. Specifically, the condition of the rural poor was enhanced by progressive strategies of socialist education, starting with a basic literacy campaign in the early years and at last to free access to high school and post-secondary level education.

As a result of the priority placed by the administration of the Revolution on education, training and science, Cuba boasts a very high share of the entire Latin American region's pool of scientists and technicians. At only 2 percent of the population, Cuba is home to 12 percent of the region's scientists (Levins, 2008:129).

While the Revolution brought many benefits and improvements to the lives of Cuba's agricultural workers, until recently their welfare still lagged behind those of workers in other sectors of the economy. Wages for state-based agricultural occupations before the Special Period were still the lowest of seventeen occupation categories (Diaz Gonzalez, 1999:135). The poor pay for agricultural workers was just one social barrier to agriculture production that met the requirements of both economic and human development. It is important to remember that Cuba's old model of agriculture was plagued by a number of social contradictions that restricted the workers in forming a social relationship to the land as well as to their labour and to the product of their labour. From the perspective of labour, the Soviet-inspired model of socialist agricultural development retained (albeit in a vastly altered form) an unequal social division of labour between agriculture and industry and between mental and physical labour: a division inherent in capitalist agricultural development and society. For example, on Soviet state farms, as well as the Cuban farms that were based on the Soviet model, there was an impassable chasm between management, planning and decision-making on the one hand and the labour process in the fields on the other. Despite the major inroads made in improving the general conditions of life for the rural population, socialist agriculture in Cuba from the inception of the Revolution to the late 1980s was a far cry from a form that would see the full human development of the rural work force.

Agriculture in the Special Period: The impact of the crisis and strategic responses

The collapse of the U.S.S.R. in 1992 precipitated a massive economic crisis in Cuba that is known as the Special Period in the Time of Peace, referring to a societal crisis of war-time-like proportions that ushered in a series of drastic changes in the material conditions faced by the Cuban Revolution and Cuban society. The Special Period led to another transformation of Cuba's socialist agriculture.

The crisis of the Special Period sparked a society-wide process of renovation within Cuban socialism aimed at transcending accumulated contradictions and tensions that had arisen in Cuban social, economic and political life since the Revolution. Particular attention was paid to the overbearing role that the Soviet Union played in Cuban social and economic development. Much of this influence has now receded into the background in favour of indigenous socialism better suited to dealing with the new reality faced by the country.

This crisis shook the Cuban system to its foundations and propelled the growth of a civil society. It also strengthened a hegemonic current within the PCC which sought to re-invigorate Cuban socialism in the face of drastically changed historical conditions. These transformative changes included:

- reforming the electoral system to allow for direct election of members to the national assembly and to endow the local levels of *poder popular* with greater responsibility and power;
- creating structures such as agricultural cooperatives that allowed for more workers' power in the workplace;
- reorienting production with the aim of ecological sustainability, and in the process, transforming agriculture, power generation, recycling, tourism and science itself[8]; and
- confirming socialism as the only pathway towards independence and just development.

The dominance of Soviet-inspired approaches to agrarian policy, agronomic sciences and national agricultural strategies came to an abrupt end as Cuba's system of heavily industrialized agriculture came crashing to a halt in the early years of the Special Period. The situation presented an opportunity for the development of a novel alternative approach to socialist agriculture, which coalesced out of uniquely Cuban approaches to the agrarian question. These included a swing towards new forms of production that could begin to mend the "metabolic rift" in Cuban agriculture. The new thinking refocused efforts to develop cooperatives and diverse levels of associated production; to emphasize changing patterns of land use in overcoming the urban-rural contradiction (for example, urban and peri-urban agriculture); to introduce an even stronger emphasis on the importance of small-scale production and of indigenous knowledge and skills; and finally, to develop new forms of agriculture that are better suited to producing socialist human development.

The crisis of the Special Period led to a broad debate about the effectiveness of alternative forms of development. An awareness of environmental ethics that was brought about through public education led to a change in mindset for Cubans regarding the environment, one that placed humans at the *centre* of such development (Stricker, 2007:1). The turn towards an ecological socialist agriculture fed into a broad process of social change and the transition towards a more ecologically sustainable form of socialist economy and the greening of Cuban society in general (Saney, 2003:187).

The agrarian crisis sparked by the initial shock of the Special Period exposed food security and food sovereignty as glaring "Achilles' heels of the revolution," weaknesses which had long been masked by Cuba's agricultural-export relationship with the U.S.S.R. (Madea & Rosset, 1994). Prior to the crisis, only 44 percent of national arable land was devoted to domestic food production, with output levels supplying less than half of total calories consumed nationally. The other half of total calories consumed were accounted for by food imports. Many staples in the Cuban diet were almost entirely imported (Wright, 2009:64).

With the onset of the Special Period, Cuba lost the ability to import sufficient levels of agricultural goods to feed the population. At the same time it lost access to imports of sufficient agricultural inputs, such as fuel, agrochemicals, machines and spare parts, irrigation systems, animal feed, veterinary medicines and so on, required to keep its system of agriculture functioning. As Wright notes (in Romard, 2014:148) Cuban agricultural production entered a state of severe crisis as output in the sector decreased by over 50 percent from 1989 to 1994. Domestic production of some staple foods, such as rice and root vegetables, fell to new lows by 1994, while the nation was producing "69 percent less pork, 89 percent less powdered milk, and 82 percent fewer chickens" in 1992 than it did in 1989. Even the national fish catch was cut roughly in half, from 1071 tonnes in 1986–90 to 571 tonnes in 1991–1995 (148).

Cuba's agricultural-export dependence on the Soviet Union now left production capacity of food crops for domestic consumption severely atrophied. Rather than investing in national food production for self-sufficiency, the bulk of foods had been imported using the proceeds of Cuba's foreign trade arrangements. As a result, the sudden collapse of the agroexport model led to great difficulties in providing food for the Cuban people. Malnutrition, a scourge in the countryside before the Revolution, but unknown for the better part of three decades, made a painful return. From 1989 until 1993, the most severe period of shortage, consumption of food on the island fell 30 percent, causing the average Cuban to lose thirty pounds as a consequence (Nieto & Delgado, 2002:47). The FAO office in Cuba estimated a 40 percent average drop in consumption of protein, a 64 percent decrease in fat intake and a 67 percent drop in the intake of vitamins A and C from 1999 to 1993. Another study, done in 1990 in Havana, reported that "the number of people having lunch decreased from 90 percent to 60 percent," with a decline in snacking from 64 to 42 percent (Romard, 2014:106).

Situations of agrarian crisis and food shortage in a capitalist economy can translate into windfall profits for agribusiness and finance corporations on the one hand and starvation on the other. In Cuba, while the food security situation was very tenuous in the early 1990s, there was no mass starvation, and those with special needs such as children, the sick and the elderly were prioritized for certain key goods by way of the rationing system. Decisive actions were immediately taken by the state and many organizations of civil society to prevent famine from occurring and to soften the worst impacts of the food crisis. The state's responses to the crisis were tempered at all levels by the socialist goals of preserving independence, pursuing development with social justice and ensuring provision of the basic needs of all Cuban citizens. Socialist agriculture in Cuba allowed for a swift and effective alteration of agrarian policies to suit the new conditions of the Special Period.

It also meant that the response of the state focused on ensuring that the Cuban people had access to safe, secure and sustainable nutrition, as opposed to the profit-driven short-term interests of capital. That there was no private property or private sector in agriculture, or in the production and distribution of agricultural inputs, meant that substantial steps could be taken with relative ease and that these could transform Cuban agriculture to match the changes in material conditions. At least this could be done with ease compared to any attempt at this in a capitalist nation, where the interests and power of private capital form an unassailable barrier to the restructuring of agricultural production.

With much of Cuba's industrial agriculture out of commission or severely impeded by lack of fuel, chemicals, feed and spare parts for machinery, those in the Cuban scientific community and the ecological movement who advocated an alternative approach to socialist agriculture were able to gain the attention of those in positions of power. The process of ecological reorientation of Cuban agriculture, underway in the 1980s (with the plan to eliminate chemical pesticides in favour of integrated pest management and biological pest controls in non-sugar agriculture) was accelerated by the new material conditions.

The agrarian crisis imposed the dire necessity of operating a national system of agriculture and sufficient food production for domestic consumption without use of large amounts of fuel for machinery and irrigation and without agrochemicals such as fertilizers for growing high-yield varieties. The new system had to function without the pesticides, fungicides and herbicides which had been used to protect monocultural production from its inherent vulnerabilities to weeds, pests and pathogens. As a consequence, an alternative approach to agriculture emerged on the following bases:

- a new round of agrarian reform laws aimed at decentralizing the state sector, transforming former state enterprises into worker-owned cooperatives and creating a network of enterprises at varying levels of association;
- a strategy for conducting low input agriculture crafted by state officials, scientists and farmers that advocated a transition to a more ecologically rational form of agriculture. This resulted in national-level state policies that promoted the study and extension of agroecology;
- the emergence of a national urban agriculture strategy aimed at establishing cities as centres of major food production, with enterprises organized as worker cooperatives;
- a greater role for smallhold farming (socialized in the form of cooperatives) in national food production and in production of several important export crops such as tobacco; and
- a strong role for smallhold farmers themselves, via the Asociación Nacional

de Agricultores Pequeños (National Association of Small Farmers, or ANAP), as agents and propagators of an agroecological approach to farming.

A form of socialist development has emerged in Cuba that is oriented towards producing a high level of human development as both a means of promoting further socioeconomic development and as the goal of socialist revolution. Three desired transformations in Cuban agriculture motivated these changes: 1. an agroecological revolution that dramatically improved the social conditions of agricultural producers and workers; 2. the cooperativization of the state farm sector in a turn away from the state towards the Unidades Básica de Producción Cooperativa (Basic Units of Cooperative Production, or UBPC) as a new form of social organisation; and 3. the democratization of the countryside in the form of decentralized governance and local development; this shifted decision-making about production and distribution to local communities and cooperatives.

The significance of these changes, and the fundamental role that the UBPCs play in them, is described by the Cuban social scientist Díaz Gonzalez in the following terms:

> The creation of the UBPC constituted a step forward in the process of democratization of the Cuban countryside that was initiated with the First Agrarian Reform Law of 1959. It has created greater potential for a transition towards sustainable rural and agrarian development in Cuba, by making possible a more direct form of participation of producers themselves in decision-making, making them protagonists in their own process of development. (2004:156)

Socialist agriculture in Cuba needed to be — and to some extent is still being — transformed so that it is capable of presenting its labour force with an avenue to increased levels of human development. This is not simply for the purpose of advancing human development for its own sake and as a matter of socialist principle, but also because, as the transition towards socialism advances, agricultural labour will seem less rewarding compared to other activities and will be less likely to attract committed, creative workers that are well educated and trained. This is already a major problem and a matter of concern for the leadership.

Today Cuban agricultural workers and farmers enjoy a relatively higher standard of living than their urban counterparts and tend to be highly educated and well trained, especially when compared to other rural work forces in the region. Some 100,000 people attend some form of training course related to agroecology each year, while a thousand attend a university or graduate level course (Garcia, 2002:95). The "voluntary self-initiated applications to enrol in agroecological programs" when the program was first offered in 1995 were ten to twenty times higher than other areas of study (95). Even so, due to the high knowledge requirements for agroecological production, the industry is susceptible to a lack of skilled labour characteristic of the modernization process of socialist development. The high requirements for specialized labour-power by agroecological farming also means that it can contribute to the re-population of rural areas by creating rewarding work in agriculture, and that it draws urban residents back to the countryside. Agroecology makes farming a more attractive occupation by boosting the incomes of farmers due to raised production, while also reducing the costs of inputs drastically. Adoption of an agroecological system, a thought-intensive form of production, transforms agricultural labour into a highly skilled form of labour that requires direct producers to possess advanced levels of education and training. Agroecological socialist agriculture enhances the potential for socialist human development by means of the education and training of farmers and by the adoption of participatory methods for research and extension of technology into the labour process itself. Thus, the agroecological transition contributed to the humanization of agriculture in Cuba, making it a materially and morally rewarding form of work that promotes new opportunities for the fuller development of human potential.

Agriculture and gender

Another critical dimension of human development in agriculture is the participation of women in both production and management. One of the earliest transformations brought about by Cuban socialism was the increased participation of women in the labour force, particularly, as discussed in Chapter Five, in the service sector (education, medical and legal workers) and the professions (teachers and research-ers, doctors and medical researchers and other professionals, such as lawyers). Women have long dominated jobs in these sectors in Cuba. As we have seen, this demonstrates how gender equality was brought about by Cuba's education system and is a feature of Cuban socialism that is well known. Perhaps more surprising is the increased participation of women in agricultural occupations that until recently remained male enclaves. Statistics released in April 2014 by the ANAP reveal that the participation of women who have joined agricultural production in the past few years of economic reform in Cuba, and as the movement of agricultural cooperatives grows, has increased to nearly 66,000. The same statistics show that an increased number of women farmers has gone hand in hand with the growing participation of women in the management positions of various agricultural cooperatives. An example of the significant role played by women in the agricultural sector can be found "in central Villa Clara province, where 52 percent of professional leaders in farms are women." This was noted by Neisy Santos, a woman who leads the farmers' organization in the province. She is one of four women currently heading the *campesino* movement in four Cuban provinces.[9]

Conclusion

Sustainable human development has four major dimensions: economic, social, livelihoods and the environment. In the case of the environment, Cuba's experience has provided important lessons regarding socialist human development of agriculture. Historically, agriculture has served both capitalism and socialism as a source of cheap surplus labour and a lever of economic development, generating rural social conditions that lagged significantly behind those in the rapidly growing cities. Better urban conditions have often served as a force of attraction for youth and the most productive sector of the economically active population, which, compounded with simultaneous forces of repulsion working on agricultural workers and their communities, have made urban centres irresistible. The transformation of agriculture from state enterprise and centralized planning into cooperativism and decentralized local development,[10] together with the advance in human development and an agroecological revolution, has changed the rural-urban development equation in Cuba, promising a resolution of the age-old counterposition of both capitalist and socialist development, and also solutions to the fundamental issue of food insecurity.

8. Updating the Model

More than ever today the principal task is the economic battle ... because on it depends the sustainability and survival of our social system

— *Raúl Castro, Closing Session of the Ninth Congress of the*
Unión de Jóvenes Comunistas, April 4, 2010

Cuba's economic battle

While Cuba's achievements in social, or human, development have been widely acknowledged and justly celebrated, the country's long economic battle is a different matter. In fact, it could be argued that the government under the leadership and command of Fidel Castro failed in a concerted effort fully to develop the country's forces of production within a socialist system. Although Cuba's socialist model eliminated the scourge of extreme poverty and also achieved a substantial degree of social equality in the distribution of the social product and a surprisingly high level of social development,[1] five decades of experimentation with diverse economic policies yielded more problems than solutions. In spite of its impressive achievements in social development, Cuba remains an underdeveloped economy, unable to provide its population with the income and other means of sustaining a standard of living that reflects the productive resources available to it.

In this situation what is required, arguably, is not just an update of the model (as proposed in the Report prepared for the Sixth Congress of the PCC in April 2011), but a closer look and a critical examination of the policies pursued over five decades of economic development under Fidel Castro's leadership: an unflinchingly critical evaluation of Cuba's economic battle that takes stock of the mistakes made over the years and a socialist strategy that corrects these mistakes.

The various shifts in strategy and economic policy over fifty years of the Revolution have been described, and to some extent evaluated, by economists such as Mesa-Lago from both a social scientific and ideological standpoint. Economic policy has of course been debated over the years by Cuban economists and other socialist scholars as well. However, these scholars for the most part have failed to come to terms with the weight and extent of the structural problems and obvious mistakes made by the Cuban leadership over the years. Fidel Castro is not immune from criticism, at crucial junctures having ignored advice of constructive critics from both within and outside the country on specific policy and on the whole policy framework and economic model.

With the possible exception of Zimbalist and Brundenius (1989), there appears to be a relative consensus among foreign scholars on periodizing shifts in economic policy within the Revolution. Most Cuban scholars generally follow the same periodization but stress the continuity of the process rather than its discontinuities. With an emphasis on major shifts in government economic policy as well as certain discontinuities Mesa-Lago (2000:173) identifies seven major shifts in economic policy from 1959 to 1996 (and we can add two more).

- 1959–60. From the capitalist market to a socialist state.
- 1961–63. Orthodox central planning.
- 1963–64. The Great Debate between Guevarism and economic orthodoxy.
- 1964–69. Revolutionary consciousness and human socialist development.
- 1970–85. Return to orthodoxy.
- 1986–90. The rectification campaign.
- 1990–96. Crisis and structural adjustment to forces of change in the Special Period.
- 1997–2007. Economic recovery, holding the socialist line with structural dualism and austerity.
- 2008–11. A period of structural reform, or updating the model.

Within the framework and as an extension of the socialization strategy initiated as early as May 1959, arguably the first serious mistake made by Fidel that had negative consequences for Cuba's economic development, was the Revolutionary Offensive of 1968, in which the government closed down fifty thousand small businesses. The leadership fell into an interpretation not uncommon at the time among socialist theorists, that of confusing capitalism with private enterprise and the market. As a result, any remaining vestiges of private enterprise were eliminated in one fell stroke. These small businesses were in vital personal services and in trade sectors; they were never replaced by the state, leading to a decline in service provision and the quality of life. Cubans ended up having to line up in long queues for under-supplied local stores. The government authorized a partial re-opening of the private sector and the market in the agricultural sector, but, citing widespread corruption, the government later ordered them closed down. Raúl's administration reopened them in 2007, but not before a decade in lost production, self-employ-ment and essential services that the state could not provide. Of course, hindsight is 20/20 and the government did have to contend with counterrevolutionary forces in this private sector as well as widespread corruption. In retrospect, the policy of closing down small businesses such as restaurants and trades operating in neighbourhoods and local communities was made as a result of equating small business and local markets with capitalism.

Another mistake made, it would seem, without popular consultation and against the advice of prominent scholars and even closest advisors, was to launch the Cuban economy on a path of monoculture dependence. Begun barely a year after the Revolutionary Offensive of 1968, the population was mobilized to produce ten million tonnes of sugar in the 1969–70 harvest. The target was not achieved and the effort dislocated the economy in the process. Leading the country along a path of monocultural dependence and failing to diversify production, the strategy led to an over-dependence on the U.S.S.R. for the export of sugar and the import of oil. Most significantly, this strategy led to the need to import food, at first from the Comintern and, after the collapse of the U.S.S.R., from the U.S. and elsewhere. By 2008 up to two-thirds of Cuba's supply of agricultural goods and essential food products was imported, making the economy highly susceptible to changing foreign conditions. When the global food crisis hit in 2008, resulting in rapidly increasing food prices, Cuba's food security was particularly threatened.

The structural problems that came with the failure to diversify production and to expand Cuba's markets for export, and the vulnerability that came with dependence on essential food imports, were deepened by the strategy of using tourism as a means of acquiring foreign exchange. Although it was undoubtedly dictated by circumstances and conditions over which the government had little or no control, the strategy turned out to be a two-edged sword. Tourism became a significant source of desperately needed reserves of hard foreign currency. This was gained at the major social cost of generating a seriously distorted dual economy and a major social division between those in the tourist industry with access to U.S. dollars and most Cubans with a much lower consumption capacity and standard of living. Migrant remittances had become another source of hard currency in Cuba, but this was used for consumption by Cuban family members rather than by the government to finance needed imports. A result of the tourism strategy was that a waiter in the tourist industry might have an income and purchasing power from five to ten times greater than that of an urban professional, such as a doctor or a teacher. Of course, money did not have the same meaning in socialist Cuba as it did in capitalist countries. The bulk of Cubans' basic needs could be satisfied with access to little money and the culture was not geared to increasing material consumption. Nevertheless, the structural distortion and social problems generated by the two-currency economy were serious and deep and were admitted to be so by the government itself.

The 1989–96 crisis was so severe precisely because of the economy's total dependence on the exchange of sugar for U.S.S.R. oil, and a reliance on outdated imported production technology and on the import of agricultural products and manufactured goods. In addition, with domestic production geared to the provision of inputs for the tourist industry, and with a large part of the population excluded from local markets and therefore suffering from poverty, structural and social problems of low consumption were worsened. With a dysfunctional state sector and an overly reduced small private sector in agricultural production, the structural problems of the Cuban economy were deepened and social conditions worsened, leading to problems that, by the time that Raúl Castro replaced his brother as Head of state, had begun to reach crisis proportions.

The structural problems outlined here, and debated at length by the PCC at its Sixth Congress in 2011, are not the whole extent of the problems faced by Cuba in its economic battle. Other areas of concern include a misallocation of human resources (architects becoming bellboys and professors becoming taxi drivers); the lack of a diversified economy with resiliency to cope with the inevitable economic cycles endemic to the world capitalist market; a failure to incorporate information technology advances into the economic structure; and problems related to educational and professional training programs. These problems are far-reaching, entrenched as they are in the economic structure of Cuban society as a result of a deficient economic model and some erratic and at times ill-advised policy decisions. Neither the Cuban people who have to live with these problems, nor the cause of socialism and human development, would be well served by a failure to confront this issue.

The meaning of Raúl's reforms: 2008–2011

With an economy that is socialist in form but at the same time open to the world economy, Cuba can be seen as a special case of national development. At issue in current debates on this development is finding a means to protect Cuba's socialist economy (with its universal social services and level of equality unparalleled in the capitalist world) from the forces of capitalist development and neoliberal globalization at work in the world economy. These forces are a constant in the capitalist development process but tend to expand and acquire a particular virulence in situations of crisis, to which capitalism is subject. The crisis of the early 1990s was of a different order. It was brought on not by the contradictions of the socialist system in Cuba, but by the collapse of socialism in the Soviet Union and Eastern Europe. As with capitalism, the response to crisis was to restructure the system and adjust to the forces of change that were out of Cuba's control.

Fidel's regime managed to navigate its way out of the crisis by adopting a number of market reforms. But these reforms were not system-changing. They did not undermine the fundamental pillars of the system or force the government to abandon its commitment to socialism or a socialist system, which had been adopted to meet the basic needs of the population and provide universal social services and subsidized rations. Although the coverage of the *libreta* was reduced by as much as 40 percent, placing at least 20 percent of the population at risk or below the income poverty line, not one school or clinic was closed. The system of universal social services, although strained, was kept more or less intact. However, the economic reforms that were introduced have not redressed some fundamental structural problems of the Cuban system. These structural faults have generated problems that have plagued the system ever since and that by some accounts (see Mesa-Lago & Vidal, 2010) surfaced and were magnified by the recent so-called "global financial crisis."

The change in leadership in 2008, precipitated by Fidel Castro's illness, brought Raúl Castro to the fore. He almost immediately set about adjusting the economy to the forces of change in Cuba's international relations, and, more importantly, he worked to tackle the structural problems of the economy by updating the model.

These structural problems, by many accounts, include: 1. overly centralized state planning, which had been extended to sectors such as agriculture and services that are best left to the market and the small business private sector; 2. a failure to incorporate computer-based information technologies into the production process and to initiate thereby an internal restructuring process based on the technological conversion of the country's production apparatus; 3. monoculture in economic production (reliance in early years on the export of sugar, and in recent years on tourism) and an associated failure to diversify the economic structure of production; and 4. dependency and over-reliance on imports of food and energy. In conditions of the global food crisis that hit the world capitalist system in 2008, this dependency had a serious negative economic impact on Cuba. Although government policy more or less insulated the population from sharp price hikes for food and from having to import up to 80 percent of the country's staple food supply at world market prices (versus 50 percent in 2004), the 2008 global food crisis had a major impact on the country's deteriorating balance of payments. And this was at a time when the government was struggling to cope with the fallout from the exposure of the economy to the global financial crisis.

In response to these and other structural problems in the economy Raúl announced a new cycle of economic reforms. At issue in these reforms was whether Cuba could hold to its socialist line of national development by updating the model, or if it would be forced by circumstance and pressures beyond its control to abandon socialism, or at least move the economy in a capitalist direction, as China and Vietnam did. Would Cuba decide to adopt a system of mixed economy that combines centralized government planning with elements of a market economy? In Cuba's case, this would be under the command of a socialist state that would continue to hold the socialist line and to regulate the market economy to prevent the emergence of capitalism.

The scope of the 2008–2010 reform process

When Fidel Castro fell ill the popular sport among foreign observers was renewed with vigour. Much air-time was devoted to speculations about what would happen to Cuba once Fidel Castro stepped down from the helm of state power. In retrospect, however, what struck — and in some corners, disappointed — observers was how smooth the transfer of power was. "Unity at home" was considered the "best defence against the only external power Cuba still regards as a threat, the United States."

These are not the words of a revolutionary or a Cuba-supporter, but of Julia Sweig, an academic spokesperson for the Corporate Global Empire.

"None of what Washington and the [Cuban] exiles anticipated," Sweig wrote, "has come to pass." Even as Cuba-watchers speculated about how much longer the ailing Fidel would survive, Sweig observed, "the post-Fidel transition is already well under way. Power has been successfully transferred to a new set of leaders, whose priority is to preserve the system while permitting only very gradual reforms." In this context, Sweig noted, "Cubans have not revolted, and their national identity remains tied to the defense of the homeland against U.S. attacks on its sovereignty." She added, "Not one violent episode in Cuban streets; no massive exodus of refugees … a stunning display of orderliness and seriousness." She concluded that, "despite Fidel's overwhelming personal authority and Raúl's critical institution-building abilities, the government rests on far more than just the charisma, authority, and legend of these two figures. Indeed, [Cuba] is a functioning country with highly opinionated citizens … Although plagued by worsening corruption, Cuban institutions are staffed by an educated civil service, battle-tested military officers… and a skilled workforce." Moreover, "Cuban citizens are highly literate, cosmopolitan, endlessly entrepreneurial, and by global standards quite healthy" (Sweig, 2007).

Apart from this issue of a peaceful transfer of power, Cuban journalist Manuel Yepe pointed out, "the Cuban Revolution [since the transfer of power from Fidel to Raúl] has been characterized by its pragmatism within the context of very firm ethical principles" (2008). The ability to "correct errors and negative tendencies, without losing sight of the fundamental path," Yepe noted, "has been a big factor in the survival of the Cuban vision of social revolution, which for a half century has faced very complex tests in the midst of great dangers."

Yepe is almost certainly correct in this view of the Cuban Revolution: that its resilience and survival is based on a continuous process of reform and adjustment to changing conditions as well as on a healthy and active internal debate. Raúl Castro, upon assuming office in 2007, initiated another round of internal debates on the direction of the Revolution, a debate that resulted in another round of reform measures (called "Raúl's reforms"), the meaning of which has engaged the attention of Cuba-watchers both within and without the country. Some of the reforms were announced publicly, eliciting the most diverse interpretations; others — as documented by Yepe in his review of recent and ongoing reforms to Cuba's food production process — were introduced without fanfare and elicited few comments by outside observers, who come in all kinds of ideological shades.

Wage and income reforms: 2010–2013

Under the *Labour and Social Security Resolution 9* (*LSC Resolution 9*) — signed in February 2008, although not published in the official Gazette — the limits placed on a state employee's earnings were lifted. State television reported on April 10, 2008, that for the first time in decades, there would be no limits on employees' earnings. "For the first time it is clearly and precisely stated that a salary (or wage) does not have a limit: that the roof of a salary [will] depend on productivity," reported economic commentator Ariel Terrero, with reference to new policy measures designed to improve the country's economic performance and to revamp the state wage system and create more incentive by allowing workers to earn as much as they could.

Currently the state controls about 90 percent of economic activity in Cuba and employs the vast majority of workers, often setting wages from offices in Havana. Cuba has prided itself on its relatively flat pay-scale system, ensuring a relatively equal distribution of the social product and national income. Income ranges from four to one, top to bottom, against a range of twelve to eighteen to one that prevails elsewhere in Latin America. However, Cuba's egalitarian approach has come under fire in recent years. It is held responsible for limiting production. "One reason for low productivity is there is little wage incentive and this breaks productivity and stops bigger salaries," Terrero said. The *LSC Resolution 9* aimed to break the cycle, and yet continue to respect the socialist principle, "to each according to his work, from each according to his ability." Upon taking over from an ailing Fidel in February that year, Raúl Castro promised to allow wages to reflect one's work better, a major complaint of the population. "It is our strategic objective today to advance in an articulate, sound and well-thought-out manner until the wages recover their role and everyone's living standard corresponds directly with their legally earned incomes."

Raúl Castro also launched a major reform of the agricultural sector to create conditions for state and private farmers that would allow them legally to earn as much as they could from their efforts after meeting state quotas. It is an old problem. "There is no reason to fear someone earning lots of money if it really is due to their work," Adalberto Torres, a Havana retiree, is reported to have said. "It is the same with farmers. Give them land, let them work, it is not important how much they make. It is good because it means they are producing" (Frank, 2008).

In addition, the ban on the sale of computers, DVD players, other consumer goods and cellphones and limits on Cubans staying at tourist hotels were also lifted. However, the problem here was that the vast majority of Cubans lacked the purchasing power to consume these goods or take advantage of the new opportunities for increased material consumption. One strategy of the Cuban government since the 1990s was to obtain foreign currency through their citizens who receive monetary gifts from relatives abroad. Behind this problem is the dual currency system instituted in the context of the Special Period.[2] When the fall of the Soviet Union plunged Cuba into its worst crisis in the early 1990s, President Fidel Castro bitterly announced that the U.S. dollar would become legal tender alongside the Cuban peso. He said at the time that the government had no choice but to do this and that it would allow Cuban socialism to survive, in spite of the inequality and social problems the dual currency would create.

As a result of the dual currency system and economy, the goods and services made available could only be purchased by Cubans who had the hard currency to pay for them in convertible pesos, or CUCs, which were worth twenty times more than the Cuban pesos, which most wages and salaries are paid in.[3] By putting these goods and services on legal sale, it would make life easier for those Cubans with access to CUCs, which are pegged at US$1.08. But it also brought out inequalities in a country where the average wage is equivalent to about US$17 a month.

Mayra Espina Prieto, a Cuban academic who specializes in issues of social inequality, notes that Cuba's Gini Index of income inequality rose from 0.24 in 1986 to 0.38 in 2000 (where perfect equality = 0, total inequality = 0.99) (Espina Prieto 2004). Since educaton and healthcare are universal and free in Cuba, the Gini coefficient typically underestimates the country's social equality. Cuba's score on the Gini Index is considered to have risen since 2000. Despite the dearth of updated figures, Cuba's standing remains above its neighbours in Latin America, which lie overall between 0.50 and 0.60 on the index of income distribution.

While professionals such as doctors and teachers have very low state salaries, there are Cubans with access to dollars who have considerably higher purchasing power. These people receive remittances from family members overseas, or tips from tourists, or they run small businesses, go on government missions abroad, receive CUC bonuses, or they are those who sell goods on the black market.

Currency reforms: May 29, 2008

The dual currency policy was undoubtedly functional and perhaps necessary at the time of the Special Period; in fact it probably meant survival during that time. However, it had an exceedingly high social cost in generating forms of social inequality — even a class divide — which placed a serious strain on one of most fundamental principles of socialism and the Revolution. Thus it was inevitable that the dual currency system would be dismantled when conditions allowed. Osvaldo Martinez, President of the Commission for Economic Affairs of the Cuban National Assembly, on a state visit to Madrid, acknowledged the problem and expressed a plan to abolish the dual currency system. "The government's policy is elimination of the dual currency, which in some way hurt the national self-esteem, but we need a minimum of monetary reserves for a normal exchange rate." The government did not propose to eliminate the peso, the national currency, because it lacked the foreign reserves to back and circulate only CUCs. The U.S. dollar, which circulated in Cuba from the mid-1990s on was removed from circulation late in 2004 because of the growing class divide and social discontent that it spawned. Today whenever a dollar is converted into CUCs, the government charges a 10 percent tax, which provides a minimal addition to the government's fiscal resources.

Pension reform: April 27, 2008

Barely two weeks after the announced labour code reform, the government under the new regime announced a policy to reform the pension system. In a 2008 speech, Raúl Castro declared that one of the Revolution's invariable principles was to raise workers' wages and pensions, starting from those with the lowest, in the effort to reduce social inequalities and to reach a point where all Cubans were able to live off their work or pensions. Needless to say, the pension system, like the ration card, no longer fully supported this principle, the value of pensions having been significantly reduced over a decade and more of economic adjustments to the new economic reality. The announced reform was designed to compensate for this loss in value using fiscal resources made in five years of recovered export-led growth. In 2008, the Revolutionary government announced that it had "decided to increase social security and assistance pensions, in a fair acknowledgement to millions of men and women who have devoted a large part of their lives to creative work over nearly 50 years of building a new society and who are still firmly defending our socialism" (Raúl Castro, 2008b)

The government decided to increase the wages of workers in the courts and public prosecutors' offices. In 2005, economic realities (three years of economic growth) allowed income increases for more than five million workers, retirees and people dependent on social security and assistance: almost 50 percent of the population. At the time Cubans were informed that, "as economic realities, the fruit of hard work, savings, productivity and efficiency ... wages and pensions would continue to increase." Wage and salary raises were designed and applied by sector and priority, always with "a rigorous assessment of economic and financial conditions as a premise for their implementation." Thus, the government noted in its announcement that, for that reason "it is not currently possible to apply across-the-board wage increases, as the country does not as yet have the necessary resources."

The improvement in pension benefits came into effect on May first and covered all social security retirees receiving pensions of up to 400 pesos monthly, more than 99 percent of the total. The minimum social security pension was also increased, from 164 to 200 pesos; retirees receiving pensions of 202 to 360 pesos received a 40-peso increase; and those on pensions of 361 to 399 pesos received 400 pesos. Families covered by social assistance received an increase of 25 pesos each, bringing the minimum up from 122 pesos to 147, a 20 percent increase. These increases, by the government account, benefited 2,154,426 people, almost the same number as those who received the salary raise for workers in the People's Supreme Court and the Public Prosecutor's Office.

International agencies acknowledge that more than half of the world's population still has no guarantee of social security. In Cuba social security is assumed by the state as a matter of human right, and on this basis the government channels a significant part of its fiscal resources to provide a measure of social security to the entire population, protecting people unable to work due to age, disability, sickness or maternity. In the case of the death of a worker, similar protection is guaranteed to his or her family and, by means of social assistance, to senior citizens without resources or homes, as well as all people unable to work and who do not have relatives to help them.

Together with its health and education programs, the social security provided by the state to the entire population is a major achievement of the Revolution, and undoubtedly a major cause for Cuba's high rate of human development. It is reflected in Cuba's high life expectancy and low infant mortality rates, which are equal to those of the most economically advanced countries in the world, a theoretical anomaly as well as a major policy and political achievement.

The economic realities of the Special Period put these and other achievements of the Revolution at serious risk. One of the most outstanding achievements of the Revolution was its ability to withstand the forces of change and survive a production crisis of such historic proportions with its basic structure of economic and social policies intact. Notwithstanding the enormous pressure of extremely scarce financial and economic resources, not one school or hospital was closed. Resources were stretched beyond their limits, and the requirements and pressures of economic adjustment led the government to institute reforms that themselves threatened to undo the entire system.

Back to the food production crisis: July 26, 2008

Even though there had been no major public announcements about it, nor comments by the legion of Cuba-watchers and the capitalist media, no reform has been as significant as the 2008 efforts to reform Cuba's food production system under the terms of *Decree Law 259*, touching as these reforms did on "a matter of national security for the revolutionary process" (Yepe, 2008).

This reform process and its "far-reaching economic and social scope" and implications, were compared by Yepe to the agrarian reforms of the early years of the revolutionary process. As argued above, it was a monumental mistake for the Revolutionary regime to sacrifice food security in order to gain an advantage on the capitalist world market. The resulting problems have come home to roost in the current global context of dramatically rising food prices. Food imports in 2007 cost the country US$1.6 billion, and this rose thereafter, placing serious constraints on national development and causing a local consumption crisis due to domestic food costs.

One of the most significant changes wrought by the 2008 *Decree Law 259* was to turn idle land over for use by state entities, cooperatives and any Cuban citizen physically fit for agricultural labour. The aim of the decree was to reverse the decline in the acreage of cultivated land, which had fallen 33 percent from 1998 to 2007. After the decree went into effect, farmers were brought together through their local organizations to state their needs in terms of machinery, spare parts, irrigation equipment, ploughs, windmills and other inputs needed to make the best possible use of the land.

Earlier there had been a reorganization of the agricultural sector aimed at moving decision-making as close to the fields as possible by eliminating intermediary layers. In the context of what might be described as administrative decentralization and local development, municipal representatives to the Ministry of Agriculture took over many of the functions that had been centralized, including serving private farmers and those organized in cooperatives. In addition, state food purchasing companies, which buy 70–80 percent of the crops harvested by private farmers, increased the prices for the food products they purchased (the remainder of the farmers' produce is sold directly to the public on the open market). State farms and farmers' cooperatives would presumably have experienced a similar price increase, allowing them productively to invest some of the proceeds as well as to improve the livelihoods of farm households. Farmers and farm workers are currently being remunerated for their labour at levels well above prevailing payscales in the urban centre and work under conditions that are vastly improved over those prevalent in other countries of the region.

More than a few have objected to the power that the measure cedes to private property in the context of a socialist project that theoretically is wedded to social property and that therefore would assign a minor role to individual property and market production. However, factors relating to the survival of the revolutionary process have led to a convincing case made in favour of the measure, which, as Yepe noted, in a review of the reform process "borrows elements of the market economy to use to serve a pressing socialist objective."

The ultimate aim of the food production system reform was to increase food security and contribute to national development and an improved livelihood for the farming population in Cuba. The as-yet unsettled question is whether the reform process activated by *Decree Law 259* will bring about this development, and what effect it will have on Cuba's socialist path to national development. It is also not decided which capitalist institutions should be incorporated for the sake of national development into what is still fundamentally a socialist system. Socialism or capitalism or a new composite of the two?

The private sector and employment reforms: August 2010
On August 12, 2010, Raúl Castro announced the imminence of another round of economic reforms, which were designed to absorb the surplus labour from the state sector: perhaps as many as 100,000 jobs. This became 500,000 by April 2011. The regime had already shed hundreds of thousands of state-sector jobs in previous years. The only way to manage this cut to public sector employment — without reneging on the right of all Cubans to adequately remunerated activity — was to expand the private sector. This was the aim of the round of reforms announced in August 2010 and acted upon some six months later, after extended public debate and internal discussion.

Cuba and the global capitalist financial crisis

The Economic Commission for Latin America and the Caribbean's preliminary report on the global financial crisis (ECLAC, 2009) noted that its strongest regional effects were channeled not through the financial sector but through the economy, by means of a decline in exports, commodity prices, remittances, tourism and foreign direct investment. In most of the ECLAC countries the negative impact of the crisis was minimal in that financial systems did not deteriorate, currency markets were relatively calm, and external obligations were met. The reason for this was that they were able to shield themselves. Mesa-Lago and Vidal argue that Cuba was an exception to ECLAC's observations of the region. The main reason was the symbiotic relationship in Cuba between economic growth and the external sector in the country's small and open economy.

From 2004 to 2007, Cuba's GDP increased at an annual average of 9 percent, largely due to Venezuelan trade, economic aid and price subsidies, but also due to the primary commodities boom on the world market. In this environment unemployment decreased to 1.8 percent while some social services improved. In 2008, Cuba had the highest allocations for social services in Latin America: 34.7 percent of GDP and 52.6 percent of current budgetary expenditures, up from 29.9 percent in 1989 (Mesa-Lago & Vidal, 2010:692).

The year 2007 marked a high point in four years of steady growth, but the onset of a financial crisis in 2008 in the world capitalist system, combined with three disastrous hurricanes that year, provoked seriously adverse economic and social consequences for Cuba. By the time the global financial crisis affected Cuba, the entire capitalist market system was already weakened. The rate of GDP growth decelerated from 7.3 percent in 2007 to 4.1 percent in the following year. Exports stagnated at 21 percent of GDP, and the balance of trade turned negative. External debt increased from 9.8 percent of GDP in 2002 to 15.8 percent in 2008. The fiscal deficit doubled in 2008, reaching its highest level in the decade.

As for the country's celebrated social programs, data for 2009 showed a rise in social expenditure as a percentage of total budget expenditures, mainly as a result of a significant increase in education and a minor rise in pensions, whereas the remaining service categories stagnated or decreased (Mesa-Lago & Vidal, 2010:700). Cuba's pension system was still the most liberal in Latin America: retirement ages were four years lower for women and two years lower for men than regional averages; retirement spans were the longest on average, due to the higher life expectancy. Liberal entitlement conditions, system maturity, population aging and insufficient financing pushed pension costs from 4.6 to 7 percent of GDP between 1986 and 2008. The *Social Security Reform Law*, enacted on December 24, 2008 in the midst of the crisis, addressed some but not all of these problems. The retirement age was increased by five years for both sexes: to sixty for women and sixty-five for men. This was to be phased in gradually over seven years. At the same time the number of required work years increased from twenty-five to thirty (although pensions were increased for each year that retirement was postponed) and nominal pensions were raised (Mesa-Lago & Vidal, 2010:699–700).

Between 2002 and 2006, the number of social assistance beneficiaries increased by as much as 120 percent, placing strains on the budget for social programs. Social assistance expenditures climbed and peaked at 7 percent of total social expenditures in 2006, but they fell to 4.3 percent in 2008 and to 4.1 percent in 2009, while the number of beneficiaries declined by 3 percent that year. Even so the pensions deficit rose to 41.3 percent in 2009, one year after implementation of the law (Mesa-Lago & Vidal, 2010:699–700). This is to say, Cuba's social assistance program, like the other components of the social service system, was already seriously stressed when the capitalist world's crisis hit.

Under these conditions, and given a further erosion in the purchasing value of wages, the government postponed implementation of the announced elimination of rationing to 2011. The fundamental problem was that the government's turn to the market under prevailing social conditions spelt disaster for Cubans subsisting on meagre wages, whose value had steadily declined over the decade, and for those on insufficient pensions, which were set below an unofficial but effective income poverty line. The average wage over the decade had increased from 188 to 427 pesos per month, but its real value had declined from 188 to 48 pesos. Neither a social insurance pension nor wages were sufficient to cover the basic needs of many Cubans. Even worse, the negative impact of the global financial crisis, in addition to increased restrictions imposed by the U.S. administration, reduced the amount and value of remittances, on which, it is estimated, up to a third of families were dependent for "extra" (but clearly basic) income.

Internal factors predating the crisis were also at work. There was a decrease in sales of Cuban professional services (physicians, nurses, teachers and others) to Venezuela, the main source of expansion for Cuba's services exports since 2004. These exports had initially experienced a boom based on beneficial agreements with Venezuela, but they soon stagnated due to limits on the number of health personnel that Cuba could export without seriously curbing its domestic provision. Simultaneously, other economic sectors were left behind, partly because of the low multiplier effect of professional service exports due to their poor linkages with the domestic economy, in contrast to the agro-industrial sugar and tourist sectors, which had been engines of growth in previous decades.

In addition, the Cuban economy suffered severe external shocks in 2008. The terms of trade fell 34.3 percent, the worst decline of the decade, due to the collapse of the world market price of nickel, which by then was Cuba's main export. An escalation in world prices of oil and food occurred, which were Cuba's two most significant imports. Three hurricanes caused losses estimated at US$ 9.7 billion, mainly in housing and food production, which required an increase in imports from 17.6 percent of GDP in 2007 to 23.3 percent in 2008 (Mesa-Lago & Vidal, 2010:601–05). Fiscal expenditure was affected by the damage inflicted by the hurricanes, and by the rise in world oil and food prices, which forced an increase in state subsidies on domestic prices of these goods. Cuba was already in a fragile macroeconomic situation when the global crisis hit.

The Cuban government responds to the financial crisis

An important observation that must be made of the 2008 global financial crisis was that it was not really global. It affected primarily, if not exclusively, countries at the centre of the capitalist market system. Secondly, notwithstanding the financialization of capitalist development, and the resulting disjuncture between the money and the real economy, the financial crisis had serious ramifications for the real economy and put many people at risk, both in the developed and developing worlds. Many on the periphery of the system were in dire straits, their livelihoods were jeopardized, and they were pushed into poverty.

A major debate has emerged about the scope of the financial crisis and whether or not — and under what conditions — it triggered a broader or deeper economic crisis, exacerbating the effects of environmental dimensions of the crisis. Some argued that the crisis was largely restricted to economies and societies at the centre. Economists at ECLAC, for example, argued that the region had "missed the bullet," with governments either finding ways to insulate their economies from the transmission effects, or enacting effective countercyclical policies, which minimized the effects.

Retrospective analysis confirms that the crisis was not in fact global. However, once again Cuba appears to be a special case. With an economy that in crucial respects was open to the global system, Cuba was particularly vulnerable to what economists have identified as "trade-growth transmission mechanisms," and, lacking the resources for a countercyclical expansion, it was not in a position to cushion or ward off the negative effects of the crisis. As a result, Mesa-Lago and Vidal argue, Cuba was hit harder by the crisis than other countries in the region. At the very least, the crisis forced the government structurally to adjust to changing conditions and forces released by a system in crisis. This was certainly the view of the Cuban administration of the economy at the time. This view led to the recognition of the need for an open and extended debate on the state of the economy and for an update to the model used to guide policy in the direction of national development.

The government's immediate response to the crisis was to maintain a fixed exchange rate and implement a belt-tightening policy. Cuba was not a member of any international and regional financial organizations and did not receive financial help to overcome the crisis. It had to rely on its own limited financial resources to mitigate or absorb the costs of its international exposure and to ensure necessary financial underpinning for social services.

Cuba is a special case; it is an open economy and hence vulnerable to trade-growth transmission mechanisms, but at the same time it is a socialist economy with universal social services. As emphasized by Mesa-Lago and Vidal (2010:705) in their assessment of the impact of the crisis on Cuba, "the mechanisms by which the world economic crisis [was] transmitted from developed to developing economies are conditioned by domestic factors that may attenuate or accentuate external economic shocks and their adverse social effects."

According to Mesa-Lago and Vidal, anti-crisis policies were not implemented. The reason for this, they argue, is that the state lacked the financial resources for countercyclical expansion. As a result, the government had to resort to further belt-tightening measures to rebalance the economy. It underestimated the effects of the global crisis, further complicating the financial scenario and forcing extreme adjustment measures after the fact on the expenditure side. However, the modest reforms and economic incentives to increase revenue were insufficient. Evidently, the Cuban model required more profound changes to address the crisis and provide the necessary financial underpinning for continued development and social programs.

Structural reforms in response to the crisis

On December 18, 2010, Raúl Castro, in his address to the Sixth Congress of the PCC (itself fourteen years since the previous congress) declared, "Either we correct our mistakes (*rectificamos*) or ... we sink." But rectify what, and in what direction? Does an opening towards the market mean a transition from socialism towards capitalism? On this point Raúl's answer was as follows, "Yes, there will be an opening towards the market, an opening towards capitalism."[4] Did this mean the end of the Revolution: a rupture of the socialist project? "No," he said, "it does not mean turning away from the perfect socialism of which the whole world dreams. It means the socialism that is possible in Cuba, under given conditions." Furthermore, he affirmed, "as you know the mechanisms of the market already exist in Cuban society" (Raúl Castro, 2013).

Cuba's economic model, Raúl continued, had suffered from excessive concentration in decision-making and ownership of the means of production, as well as lack of incentives and low efficiency. These problems, he noted, had impaired output and productivity and had worsened during the previous decade due to "structural weaknesses in the pattern of growth." There was, he added — harking back to the structural reforms that he had called for in 2007, reforms that would "improve production and productivity" — a "domestic consensus that the centralized state economic model had multiple shortcomings and distortions and needed profound structural changes."

The reform process: 2010–2012

The pace of the economic reform process, which began in 2008 — almost immediately upon Raúl Castro's assumption of the levers of state power — picked up again in mid-April 2011, after a Congress of the Communist Party that met to discuss the modernization of the socialist economy. Ruling out any switch to capitalism, the Congress debated a broad range of reforms, including the decentralization of government decision-making and revenue flows; allowing state-run companies more autonomy; slashing state payrolls and subsidies; and reducing the state's role in agriculture and retail in favour of a growing social, or non-state, sector.

Marc Frank (2012) provides the following chronology of reform measures adopted by Raúl Castro's government in the year leading up to this Congress (April 2010–April 2011).

- April 2010. Barbershops and beauty salons with up to three chairs went over to a leasing system. Rules for home construction and improvements were liberalized.
- June 2010. Sale of construction materials to the population was liberalized. The government authorized farm cooperatives to establish mini-industries to process produce.
- August 2010. New rules authorized smallhold farmers and Cubans with small garden plots to sell produce directly to consumers.
- The state increased from fifty to ninety-nine years the period that foreign companies could lease land as part of tourism and leisure development projects such as golf courses and marinas.
- Stores were opened where farmers could purchase supplies in local currency without regulation.
- September 2010. The government announced the lay-off of more than 500,000 state workers and awarded 250,000 new licences for family businesses, over six months. Some 200,000 of the state jobs were to go over to leasing, cooperatives and other arrangements. Unemployment benefits were cut.
- Self-employment regulations were loosened and taxes tightened. Family businesses were authorized to hire labour for the first time and to do business with the state and to rent space.
- December 2010. Raúl Castro gave his most explicit reform speech yet, urging change of "erroneous and unsustainable concepts about socialism that have been deeply rooted in broad sectors of the population over the years, as a result of the excessively paternalistic, idealistic and egalitarian approach instituted by the Revolution in the interest of social justice."
- January 2011. State banks began issuing microcredits to would-be farmers who had leased land.
- March 2011. Raúl Castro announced that the original timetable to lay off 500,000 state workers by April had been scrapped, and that there was no fixed date to complete the process. This was a result of workers' resistance to losing their jobs and balking at the high cost of proposed leasing arrangements. Castro created a new post to oversee economic reform and promoted Economy Minister Murillo to the job.
- April 2011. Authorities announced that 120,000 people had leased land since

2008 and that 180,000 people had taken out licences to work for themselves or to rent space to new entrepreneurs since the previous October.

- State banks were authorized to issue microcredits to new entrepreneurs and state bodies to do business with them.

Broadening the reform process: 2012

Having demobilized up to half a million state workers for entry into an expanded private sector of small businesses and self-employment, and having liberalized regulations for both these small businesses and for farming, in July 2012 the government adopted a new comprehensive tax code in order to loosen regulations further on some state companies and turn others into cooperatives. The plans for overhauling the tax code were announced at a session of the National Assembly, which also agreed to deepen the reform process. The new tax law would eventually require everyone to pay income and property taxes for the first time since the 1960s. According to Marino Murillo, head of the Communist Party commission responsible for implementing reforms approved at a party Congress the previous year, the new law would bring the economic model up to date and deepen the reform process. It would provide a legal framework for opening up a market economy, for a non-capitalist private sector and for expanding the cooperative sector.

Under the new law some state companies would be partially deregulated by the end of 2012. These companies, which had previously been part of various ministries, would be able to make day-to-day business decisions without waiting for government approval; they would be permitted to manage their labour relations and set prices. After meeting state contracts, they would also be able to sell excess production on the open market. The companies would also be self-financed, including the use of bank credits, and they would be expected to cover their losses rather than seeing either profit or loss go to the state. They would no longer and receive financing and subsidies from the treasury. Instead of being micro-managed by the ministries the companies would be evaluated by indicators such as earnings, the relation of productivity to salaries and their ability to meet the terms of state contracts (Frank, 2012).

Murillo also announced that 222 small-to-medium-sized state businesses would be converted into cooperatives, ranging from restaurants and produce markets to shrimp breeding businesses and transportation authorities. The cooperatives would lease state property and equipment at ten-year renewable intervals, and they would operate on a market basis, pay taxes like other companies and divide profits among members as they saw fit.

Evaluating the reform process

The reforms introduced from 2008 to 2012 provided considerable flexibility in the labour market, such as authorization to work in more than one job, elimination of wage ceilings and permission for state enterprises to set salaries based on workers' productivity. However, until the middle of 2010, these reforms, like those in the agricultural sector, did not involve a substantial modification of Cuba's economic model, which, Raúl Castro noted (2011a), was closer to the Soviet model than the market-socialist model of China and Vietnam.

The most far-reaching project for reforming the Revolution was formulated in the context of the Sixth Congress of the PCC, which, after being postponed for some years, was finally convened in April 2011, with the explicit aim of updating the model of the Cuban Revolution in response to long-standing problems that were reaching crisis proportions.

To provide some coherence and a framework for discussions of Congress delegates, a Central Report was prepared, based on an evaluation of the state of the economy and the problems to be solved, and that "took into account the major events and circumstances, both external and internal, since the [previous] Congress." Also accounted for in this report, and used as criteria for updating Cuban socialism, were the views and ideas expressed in the context of a widespread internal debate on the Cuban economy all over the country. It is estimated by February 7, more than 127,000 meetings had been held and that over seven million Cubans had participated in the analysis presented in the Project of Economic and Social Policy Guidelines of the Cuban Party and the Revolution, presented at the Sixth Congress of the Cuban Communist Party (PCC), and in the surrounding debates. These meetings, according to Raúl, provided some 619,400 proposals, deletions, additions, changes, questions and concerns. Presumably congressional delegates were also engaged in the discussions and were able to bring forth ideas in this debate and to inform discussions of the Report. A preliminary version of the Report was presented in the form of an analysis of the state of the Cuban economy presented by Raúl Castro at the closing ceremony of the Sixth Congress of the Communist Youth on April 4, 2010.

The internal conditions highlighted by Raúl and reflected in the report of the Sixth Congress included factors such as low productivity, decapitalization of the productive base of the economy and infrastructure, and an aging and stagnant population growth. External conditions included an environment of systemic and institutional crisis with multiple dimensions: economic, financial, energy, food and ecological. These had an impact that weighed more heavily on developing countries. Cuba, the Report noted, with an open economy and dependent on its external economic relations, had not been immune from the impact of the capitalist crisis. This was manifest in the price instability of the country's tradable goods, in the external demand for its social product and in restrictions in the possibility of accessing capital.

The creation of the intergovernmental organization Alternativa Bolivariana para los Pueblos de Nuestra América (Bolivarian Alternative for the Peoples of Our America, or ALBA) in 2004 shielded Cuba from these negative conditions to some extent, providing the country with new sources of revenue in the services sector, especially in health and education services. It also provided significant new opportunities for trade with other countries, especially China, Vietnam, Russia, Angola, Iran, Brazil and Argentina. Nevertheless, several structural problems, such as dependence on imported food in conditions of rising prices, created a situation in 2008 and 2009 that required the adoption of structural reforms and an updating of the model used to guide national policy. An example cited in the Report was the deterioration in Cuba's terms of trade, which declined by 15 percent between 1997 and 2009 and led to a net loss of US$10.2 billion.

In response to these conditions and in anticipation of possible foreign trade consequences, Raúl Castro suggested that the country adopt two solutions (2011b). First, short-term policy measures were needed that would eliminate the growing balance-of-payments deficit, generate export revenues and substitute for imports. These measures could also respond to problems related to work motivation and income distribution, creating the infrastructure and productive conditions that would permit an advance to a higher stage of development. Secondly, Raúl suggested that measures be taken that would bring about sustainable development in the long-term, which would allow for a high level of food and energy self-reliance, for efficient use of human resources, for heightened export competiveness in traditional products and for the production of value-added new goods and services (Raúl Castro, 2011a:7).

The resulting updated model would take the following form: 1. the system of socialist planning would continue to provide the major direction to the national economy, and to give rise to new forms of action and leadership; 2. the socialist state enterprise would stimulate the development of mixed capital enterprises, cooperatives, *usufructarios* (leaseholders), rentiers and leaseholders, self-employment and other forms that could contribute to the productivity of labour; 3. the concentration of ownership would not be permitted; and 4. the planning process would encompass not only the system of state and mixed-capital enterprises, but would also regulate non-state forms of enterprise, implying and necessitating modalities of economic planning.

As for the social policy framework the new model would: 1. preserve the major achievements of the Revolution, such as access to health services and medical attention, education, culture, social security and assistance to those in need; and 2. redeem the role of labour as the fundamental means of contributing to society and of satisfying basic personal and family needs (*personales y familiares*). In addition, the model would 3. strengthen the role and scope of wage relationships, ensuring that all forms of work and economic activity were properly remunerated in the form of a salary (reducing gratuities and subsidies), 4. gradually eliminate the *libreta* (ration card), which led to the practice of bartering and an informal underground market; 5. maintain food provision in health and education centres that need it and cafeterias where required, but assuring payment for services without subsidies; and 6. guarantee the provision of social assistance, via a coordinating centre, for persons who really needed it, because they were unable to work and had no family members to help out (Raúl Castro, 2011a:21–22).

Under these conditions and within a policy framework elaborated to the purpose, the Report to the Sixth Congress of the PCC included the reforms to the economic model of Cuban socialism outlined in the next few pages.

Self-employment

The government's reform agenda under Raúl Castro's leadership included self-employment as a matter of top priority: the reversal of the Revolutionary Offensive of 1968 when the private sector was abolished, not just in terms of capitalist enterprises, but virtually all small- and medium-sized businesses were eliminated. The aim in this self-employment reform was not only to adjust the economy to forces generated globally, or simply to effect another turn of the austerity screw, but instead it intended to correct a major error in judgement and policy. The mistake that had such enormous economic and social implications had been to conflate capitalism with market economics and private enterprise. It would take the regime more than forty years to appreciate the magnitude of the problems generated by this mistake.

What the PCC told its members in an internal document circulated for discussion at both the base and leadership levels was that when it came to *cuentapropistas,* or self-employed workers, both the party and the government must "first of all facilitate their activities and not create stigmas or prejudices against them, much less demonization." Secondly, the party was called upon to "defend the interests of self-employed persons just as we do all other citizens, provided they act in compliance with established laws." The actual formulation of relevant policy measures, by diverse accounts, was the product of an extended internal debate. Without any documented review of this debate it is not possible to know what the decisive factors were in the design of this new policy reform. It is likely that the success of similar policies in several countries that were deciding on what level of market incursion to allow in their societies — Vietnam in particular — featured in discussion and considerations. Vietnam's ruling Communist Party had implemented policies that freed farmers to market their products and allowed self-employed entrepreneurs in the cities to set up restaurants or other businesses, with the obligation to pay social security for their employees. The policy measures announced by the Cuban government in April 2011 appear to have had similar features.

To anticipate what the scope and likely consequences of this policy would be, or to predict how these consequences could be managed, was no easy task. It is no idle thing to throw 500,000 public sector workers, who had previously been completely reliant on wage or salary, onto the mercy of an as-yet non-existent market: to assume that some innate entrepreneurship of these citizens would simply kick in. For one thing, many if not most redundant state workers had absolutely no experience in small business management. Cuba had neither a supportive culture nor the institutional development of a market economy. Also, a critical factor in the development of small- and medium-sized private non-capitalist enterprises is financing, so it was clear that the government would need to assume an important role in "facilitating the transition … and the social transformation of state-sector workers into a class of self-employed entrepreneurs and small business owners, including operators of what in other contexts are defined as 'micro-enterprises.'" What shape the government's role would take, or has taken in the subsequent three years, is not clear. Even so it was evident in 2011 that the provision of credit would be a major consideration, and the government over the past three years has been working closely with an emerging non-capitalist private sector of small family businesses and with a social sector of nongovernmental organizations that have entered the fray of microenterprise lending, a practice that has had disastrous results in other parts of Latin America (Bateman, 2010).

The rationing of food and basic goods

Another keystone of the social welfare system of the Revolution, the *libreta* or ration book, was also at stake; it was probably the most highly debated issue. For some years the number of items on the *libreta* had been reduced gradually and restored to the market, but not without considerable discussion and debate. Indeed the document announcing the government's intention to do away with the *libreta* acknowledged that "many of [us] Cubans mistake socialism for entitlements and subsidies, equality for egalitarianism, and many of us consider [the ration book] a social achievement that should never be reversed." In any event the reform included incentives to subsidize not certain products but those products that "Cubans for one reason or the other really need." "Such measures" (the elimination of the ration book), the document goes on to state, and "others that will be necessary to apply, although we know they are not popular, are unavoidable and needed in order to maintain and improve the free services of public health, education and social security for all citizens." Undoubtedly, the announcement added, "the ration book and its removal spurred most of the contributions of participants in the debates, and it is only natural. Two generations of Cubans have spent their lives under this rationing system that has for four decades ensured every citizen access to basic food at highly subsidized derisory prices."

The distribution mechanism of the *libreta* introduced in times of shortages during the 1960s — in the interest of "providing equal protection to our people from those involved in speculation and hoarding with a lucrative spirit" — had become, in the course of the years, an "intolerable burden to the economy," discouraging work in addition to "eliciting various types of transgressions." "Certainly', the Report continues, "the use of the ration book to distribute basic foods, which was justified under concrete historic circumstances, has remained with us for too long, even when it [came to] contradict the substance of the distribution principle that should characterize Socialism, "from each in accordance with his ability and to each in accordance with his labour." This situation, the Report adds, "should be resolved."

On this point, the Report makes reference to "what comrade Fidel indicated in his Central Report to the First Party Congress on December 17, 1975," namely that "there is no doubt that in the organization of our economy we have erred on the side of idealism and sometimes even ignored the reality of the objective economic laws" that Cubans should comply with. "The problem," the Report added, "that we are facing has nothing to do with concepts, but rather with how to do it, when to do it, and at what pace." In this context, "the removal of the ration book [was] not an end in itself ... [but] one of the first indispensable measures aimed at the eradication of the deep distortions affecting the operation of the economy and society as a whole."[5]

On this point Raúl Castro (2013) observed, "no member of the leadership of this country in their right mind would think of removing that system by decree, all at once, before creating the proper conditions to do so, which means undertaking other transformations of the economic model with a view to increasing labour efficiency and productivity in order to guarantee stable levels of production and supplies of basic goods and services made accessible to all citizens but no longer subsidized."

One of the "other transformations" was to deal with "the mismatch between salaries and the ranking or importance of the work performed," an issue closely related to "pricing and to the establishment of a single currency, as well as to wages and to the *reversed pyramid* phenomenon. And yet another problem, that need[ed] action, relate[d] to the excessively centralized model characterizing our economy" (my emphasis).

Here Raúl Castro announced the intention of the government to "move in an orderly fashion, with discipline and the participation of all workers, towards a decentralized system where planning will prevail, as a socialist feature of management, albeit without ignoring current market trends." In this regard, he notes, "the lesson taught by practical experience is that excessive centralization inhibits the development of initiatives in the society and in the entire production line, where cadres got used to having everything decided 'at the top' and thus ceased to feel responsible for the outcome of the entities they headed."

Reflections on the reform process

The current regime has certainly made a number of fundamental concessions to capitalism, which threaten to undermine the socialist human development model that has shaped government policy and the Revolution over the years. For example, a key concession has been about how equality is conceived and instituted. The

Cuban model was based on the institution of egalitarian relations and equality as a social condition. In the updated model of the Revolution, however, there is a clear shift from a commitment to equality as a social condition — egalitarianism — towards equity, or the equality of opportunity: the social liberal, rather than the socialist, conception of equality. This latter concept is also the hallmark of the UNDP's human development model of capitalist development. However, the reforms advanced by Raúl Castro do not mean that Cuba will be forced to tread a capitalist path towards national development.

Raúl Castro's reforms, particularly the legalization and vigorous promotion of small business, is a positive step forward, providing vital services and ending a dysfunctional state apparatus, which for a half century failed in its mission of economic development. The next step will be to allow medium-sized enterprises, which employ labour, to come into operation, especially in high-tech activities, innovative manufacturing, food processing and especially in producing commodities for export. While a capitalist restoration is always possible, the current prolonged stagnation is not an option. There are several safeguards that can be adopted; several existing regulations, if effectively and fairly applied, can retain socialist predominance over the economy and society.

A professional tax and revenue agency can enforce a graduated income or revenue tax with sanctions. This could prevent the concentration of wealth and keep inequalities within bounds and socialist guidelines. Labour inspectors can oversee health, occupation and labour standards to prevent exploitation and ensure profit-making does not take place at the expense of workers. Most importantly, independent worker-elected trade unions with the power to negotiate with capital and with the right to take job action and file grievances to an independent labour board are absolutely essential. Independent workers' unions must have access to the books in order to oversee tax evasion, black market racketeering and other anti-socialist behaviour, and to report any such activity to appropriate state agencies. In addition to these regulatory controls, capitalist development could be inhibited by the lack of institutional support for the perquisites and power of private property, such as the freedom to accumulate capital by exploiting labour. Capitalism cannot function without legal protection of private owners' means of social production. Also, formation of a capitalist class requires institutional development of a market for capital.

Raúl's reforms argue for greater enterprise autonomy from central authorities and especially from party functionaries, giving priority to experts and entrepreneurs over political loyalists. This is a two-edged sword; it encourages greater skill in developing market opportunities and international agreements, but managerial autonomy could very quickly become a vehicle for the growth of a quasi-capitalist class at the peak of the economy. This has happened in China, Vietnam and Russia. But to counter capitalist tendencies at the top by heavy-handed day-to-day intervention by state-party bureaucrats would stifle the purpose of the ongoing reform process. A more meaningful option would be to promote the development of councils of workers, engineers and employees that can meet to discuss and review performance, salaries and productivity gains and obstacles, and to take decisions in line with socialist principles of equality, equity and innovation. What is needed is a more participatory form of social development. Developing entrepreneurial skills, increasing earnings and ensuring socialist values of solidarity and equality create inevitable tensions that will need to be mediated by representatives of the broader socialist society.

Above all there is a need to carry out basic reforms that go beyond immediate improvisations. Massive self-employment is no answer to the need for greater productivity, dynamic exports, sustained investments and the creation of skilled employment for an educated population. Cuba largely lost out on the commodity boom that benefited Latin America in the latter half of the last decade. Cuba needs to expand investments in the production of commodities and services for export. The country is well positioned to take advantage of five decades of productive investments in human resource development, especially in education, healthcare and medical services. However, Cuba needs to find a way of incorporating techno-logical innovations and advances in information technology into the production apparatus. At the level of international trade — a matter of critical importance to a small island economy — ALBA is an excellent staging point for advancing socialist principles of fair trade. More broadly, regarding the production of commodities for export, there is a voracious market in China as well as favourable conditions for Cuba's terms of trade. These would allow Cuba to enter the broader global capitalist market with a competitive advantage. As for technological conversion, Cuba could develop ethanol production as a substitute for imported oil (even at Venezuela's discount) using Brazilian science, importing Haitian labour and ending the irrational rhetoric from past leaders who were blind to the benefits of alternative sources of fuel and applied energy sciences, especially solar energy, which is so plentiful throughout the year.

The dead hand of the bureaucracy condemned by Raúl cannot be changed by the leading heads of the same bureaucracy. Direct producers must not merely debate and petition; they must be in a position to lower the costs of production, even if only to enhance their own earnings.

In a socialist economy, the market should not be confused with or equated to capitalism. There is room in a socialist economy for both public and private enterprise, a private as well as a public and social sector. In Cuba since 2008, market reforms have been beginning and that is a necessary and positive move, providing they are accompanied by political reforms that strengthen the countervailing power of labour, consumers and environmentalists. Raúl Castro himself has noted the insufficient representation of Afro-Cubans and women in positions of political power. Those observations and the injustices are reflected in social inequalities in society. Race and class reforms are necessary to counter the largely Euro-Cuban elite emerging at the heads of the autonomous centres of decision-making in peak economic organizations. Cuba has huge quantities of under-used land, natural resources, skilled labour, talented artists, agriculturalists and innovators.

Breaking the dead hand of the political and civil bureaucracy by means of market reforms is a step forward. To ensure that social and political development is governed by socialist principles requires workers' control over their workplaces and control by communitarians over their communities. In addition, workers and professionals, and Cubans in all walks of life, must deepen their engagement with and participation in the political process. The Communist Party has a role to play if and when it shifts from being top-down, gerontocratic and dynastic to being an open, horizontal party for people of all ages that provides a platform for debate that would give options to elected policy-makers. As argued recently by Marta Harnecker in the context of Venezuela, socialism implies democracy, but not the limited democracy advanced in the liberal democratic tradition, which often turns into the rule of capital or oligarchy.

In the meantime, Cuba needs to move decisively to diversify production and develop new lines of exports: commodities, processed foods, high-tech products and services, among others. The market exists; the skilled labour is there; the resources are available. The question is whether Cuba's leaders are ready to open up in a rational way, or whether they will to continue in the improvised fashion of past erratic swings: from sugar to tourism, from full employment to mass layoffs, from state enterprise to cooperative enterprise and self-employment.

The countervailing force to a growing private sector is not a decrepit and inefficient bureaucracy but a dynamic independent movement of workers and consumer councils in factories, offices and markets. If and when autonomous enterprises take off, they will quickly by-pass old guard statist bureaucrats, just as they have in parts of Asia. Only new class sociopolitical formations, hi-tech innovation and market and managerial savvy can provide oversight and ensure compliance with socialist norms and the protection of Cuba's advanced social welfare programs. If Cuba's past imbalance was characterized by too much welfare and not enough production, that is no reason to make the switch by sacrificing social policy to achieve high productivity gains. A more reasonable outcome can result not so much from achieving a better balance between the state and the market — the concern of the architects of the post-Washington Consensus — as seeking out a balance in power between autonomous directors and autonomous workers' organizations as they struggle over who gets what, where and how.

9. Conclusion

Since the Revolution in 1959 Cuba has been a major thorn in the side of U.S. imperialism and a source of inspiration for people and countries all over the developing world who are looking for a way to pursue paths independent of development in a world dominated by global capital. At issue for these countries is whether to do so within the confines of the dominant world capitalist system or within an alternative socialist system. The collapse in the early 1990s of existing socialism in the form of the Soviet development model seemed for many to settle the issue: socialism was dead and capitalism triumphant. But there has also been the evident fact of capitalism's propensity for crisis and class division. This is undeniable when confronted with the differences in the lives led by the financiers and the top 1 percent of the population and the lives of many if not most of the working people of the world. In addition to the workings of the capitalist system there are destructive forces released by the dominant neoliberal model of free market capitalism now in place globally. This model has proven to be highly destructive of both livelihoods and the environment, putting many people — and all life on earth — at risk. This is particularly true of the estimated 1.4 billion people deemed by the agencies of international development to be to be too poor to meet even their basic needs. Not only are they the chief victims of global capitalism and its destructive operations, but they are particularly vulnerable to crisis conditions that are generated in the process. The conditions have raised serious questions about whether capitalism is really a viable way forward. Many would prefer to lower the level of economic growth, and to see a more equitable sharing of the fruits of this development established, and also to move towards a more human form of development, This puts Cuba back in the picture as an example of socialist humanism and as a model of socialist development in the twenty-first century.

So what lessons can be drawn from the history of the Cuban Revolution? One could not look at Cuba for a model of economic policies to develop society's forces of production. In spite of its impressive and laudable achievements in social or human development, Cuba remains an underdeveloped economy. Nevertheless, the Cuban Revolution warrants a closer look, particularly with regard to its concept of human development and the search for a systemic alternative to capitalism.

The emergence in the 1980s of what was called a "new economic model" — neoliberalism — and a "new world order" — free market capitalism — signalled a new and particularly destructive advance in the history of capitalism. This was in spite of the ostensibly innocent desire to liberate the "forces of freedom" from the regulatory constraints of the welfare development state. However, the forces of change and crisis released in this process of capitalist development were so destructive that they generated powerful new forces of resistance; this in turn brought about many efforts to restructure the system in an effort to guard against the possibility that it might be abandoned. The aim, in other words, was to reform the system in order to save it from itself and its propensity towards crisis, the destruction of the planet and the degradation of all life. As outlined in this book, a number of alternative models of capitalist development have been proposed, including a model of sustainable human development advanced by economists at the UNDP. These economists believe in capitalism. They believe that its destructive forces (the imperative to accumulate, unbridled greed ...) can be tamed and that its key institutions can be reformed so as to produce a more inclusive and humane form of development.

This is precisely where the Cuban model can help. It provides empirical evidence that socialism provides a better system and a more appropriate institutional and policy framework for human development than capitalism does. The concept of human development advanced and defended by the UNDP saw capitalism as the best system to meet its system requirements. The idea was that it is possible to create a more human form of society and development if the state is brought back into the development process. This state involvement would put in place a series of institutional and policy reforms, which would include administrative decentralization. This decentralization would bring government closer to the people and allow for meaningful forms of participation in the making of decisions that affect people in their communities, workplaces and daily lives.

Again, this is where Cuba comes in, supporting the argument that capitalism — based as it is on class exploitation and a drive to accumulate wealth that overrides all other considerations — is crisis ridden and inherently inhuman, unable to overcome its built-in contradictions. The central argument of this book is that the project behind the Cuban Revolution is fundamentally different in key respects from what was understood as socialism of the twentieth century (particularly the Soviet model). The Cuban Revolution can be seen as a model of socialist human development with useful and important lessons for the project of rebuilding socialism in current conditions. One of these lessons is that the fundamental principles of socialist human development should not, and need not, be sacrificed on the altar of political expedience or advancing the forces of production. In drawing attention to this and other lessons from the Cuban revolutionary experience it is hoped that the book will contribute to opening up a debate on how to rebuild socialism in the twenty-first century.

Notes

Introduction

1. This text substitutes the more current term "solidarity" for "fraternity."
2. The word "peasant" denotes a smallhold farmer whose livelihood is based on agriculture and who lives in rural communities in developing societies. Whenever capitalism becomes the dominant mode of production the word "peasant" tends to go out of use and is replaced with "family farmer." Under capitalism, many smallhold farmers' lands are expropriated and the families move toward wage-earning in cities; their means of production is thereby removed from them. This process is called proletarianization.
3. As discussed in Chapter Eight, it was a monumental mistake for the revolutionary regime, with its sugar-for-oil export strategy, to sacrifice food security in order to gain a comparative advantage on the capitalist world market. This problem came home to roost in the 2007–08 global context of dramatically rising food prices. Food imports in 2007 cost Cuba US$1.6 billion, placing serious constraints on national development and a local consumption crisis in domestic food costs. In response, one of the first reforms introduced by Raúl Castro when he became head of state in 2008 was to confront the issue of food insecurity; he expanded conditions for agriculture and the domestic production of food for local markets and for the economy.
4. This institutionalization of democracy meant the socialization of production and the collectivisation of economic activity in the agricultural sector, as well as democratization of the state in terms of the Local Bodies of Popular Power. On these issues see, among others, García Brigos (2001) and Harnecker (1979).
5. Williamson (1990) originated the term "Washington Consensus" with his reference and discussion of ten "structural reforms" in economic policy mandated by a host of Washington-based international financial institutions, private foundations and neoliberal policy forums, as the price of admission to the "new world order." The reforms included privatization (to revert the nationalization policy), decentralization (reverting responsibility for development to local governments) and liberalization (reverting the policy of state regulation and protectionism).

1. Socialism and Human Development

1. These contradictions include the fundamental capital-labour relationship, the rural-urban relationship, the relationship between industry and agriculture, and the economic relationships among countries on the north-south divide of the global economy.
2. This concept is embodied most clearly in the UNDP's *Human Development Report* (HDR) published annually since 1990, and in its model of "sustainable human development" used by many governments as a script to guide public policy.
3. The idea of human development, like all ideas, undergoes change over time as different people add to it or re-formulate it in response to changing conditions. When conditions are right or ripe the idea can take hold and lead to action; otherwise it just withers on the vine of academic discussion. This list gives the history of the idea of human development and its transformation into action.

2. Revolution as Socialist Human Development

1. Kerala is a state in India that has been compared with Cuba as a model of human development and in having achieved a high level of human development in conditions of relatively low economic growth (Tharamangalam, 2006). Like Cuba, Kerala has become a veritable mecca for those from other low-income nations interested in social development and health advancement (Thresia, 2014).

2. Income distribution in many countries over the past three decades of free market capitalism (neoliberalism) has become increasingly skewed, with the top 10 percent of income earners taking an increasingly larger share of the nation's wealth. This is particularly the case in the U.S., where in 2012 the top decile share of total income was 50.4 percent, the highest since 1917 (Saez, 2013:121). The share of total income appropriated by the top 1 percent is even more obscene. The income of this group from 2009 to 2012, in the wake of the "global financial crisis," in which millions of Americans lost their homes and savings, grew by 31.4 percent, while the total income of the bottom 99 percent grew by 0.4 percent. In that period the income of the bottom half fell, pushing many into poverty (120). Under the same conditions but in a global context, the eighty-five richest individuals in the world, according to an Oxfam report presented at the World Economic Forum Report in Davos (Brito, 2014), have a combined income equal to that of 3.6 billion of the world's poorest. And, of course, wealth is much more concentrated than income.

3. Socialism as Revolutionary Consciousness

1. Denise Blum (2008), an American anthropologist, has made a close on-site study of the actual dynamics of the education system with regard to the inculcation of socialist ideals and revolutionary values of the new society.

4. Solidarity as a Pllar of Cuban Socialism

1. <http://www.theguardian.com/society/2014/jun/19/poverty-hits-twice-as-many-british-households> <http://www.independent.co.uk/news/uk/politics/deprivation-britain-major-new-survey-reveals-that-poverty-is-getting-worse--even-among-working-families-9547039.html>.

5. The Equality Dimension of Socialist Humanism

1. This 1968 Revolutionary Offensive could be criticized for equating capitalism with the private sector and the market, and thus going too far in the direction of the state, abolishing not only capitalism but small businesses that operated in local communities. In the context of the Special Period in the 1990s, and in an effort to resolve certain bottlenecks in agricultural production and in employment, the government was compelled to introduce a series of market reforms that restored certain forms of private enterprise.

2. My translation.

3. <http://data.worldbank.org/indicator/SH.MED.PHYS.ZS>.

4. <http://blythlnk.com/strahauge-maps/185 the patients per doctor-map-of-the-world>.

6. Development as Freedom: The Politics of Socialist Humanism

1. This social liberal conception of freedom differs not only from liberalism in its classical formulation in economic and political terms, but also from its neoliberal formulation by the members of the Pelerin Society, and embodied in the neoliberal discourse on globalization and development. See Mirowsky and Plehwe (2009).
2. Non-Cuban scholars tend to be skeptical about these channels, viewing them and neighbourhood associations such as the CDRs, as government-controlled or in service of the state.
3. Arnold August in his detailed analysis of Cuban democracy (1999, 2013) notes that unlike Venezuela, in Cuba there are no direct elections in workplace and community councils. But this does not make Cuba less democratic, simply democratic in a different (non-electoral) form.
4. On these dynamics of democratic politics in Cuba and Venezuela, see Arnold August (2013). August notes that while the Venezuelan Consejos Comunales are meant to bypass the state, the Consejos Populares in Cuba have been established to assist the municipal assemblies; they are composed of representatives to the municipal assemblies, and decentralized into several smaller Consejos Populares, to which they are accountable.
5. Fidel Castro's CDR *Speech*/YouTube (Archival video: audio of speech, in Spanish).
6. Some scholars, such as Haroldo Dilla Alfonso (cited in several studies on Cuban democracy in 1993 and 1997), changed their views on Cuban democracy from constructive criticism (from the perspective of liberal democracy) to rabid and overtly ideological opposition (on this see August, 1999:261).

7. Agricultural Change and Sustainable Development

1. According to Marx (and many scholars agree with him on this point) capitalism (which is to say, a mode of production based on the social relation of wage labour to capital) grew from a process in which direct producers, or tillers of the land (family farmers we would call them today), are separated or alienated from the land (their primary means of social production) and forced to migrate to the cities in search of paid work. Marx referred to this process as the "primitive accumulation of capital" (capital being all forms of wealth-producing resources) and "proletarianization" ("proletariat" being Latin for those who have no estate or who own nothing but their *proles*, or offspring). What is involved in this process of capitalist development is the social transformation of small landholding farmers and independent commodity producers (who work for themselves by producing goods for sale on the market) into a working class (those who have no choice but to exchange their labour-power for a working wage). Canadian and world history over the past two centuries present countless examples of this process.
2. Proponents of "dependency theory" and "monopoly capital" argue that these two fundamental contradictions of the capitalist system are also reflected in the structure of international relations, in which producers and workers on the periphery are exploited by agents of world capitalism (the multinational corporations that dominate the world economy), which are based in the "centre" of the system (the advanced capitalist countries). Exploitation in these diverse contexts refers to the extraction of surplus value from the direct producer or worker.

3. Between 1920 and 2007 the world's urban population increased from some 270 million to 3.3 billion, adding close to 450 million to the urban centres in Latin America and radically transforming the demographic structure. While in 1920 less than one-third of the world population lived in cities and other urban centres, by 1950, 41 percent of the population was urban. By 2007, cities accounted for 72 percent of the population (United Nations Secretariat 2008:3).

4. On this metabolic or ecological rift see Foster, Clarke & Yorke (2011).

5. When at the helm of the INRA (Instituto Nacional de Reforma Agraria), Che Guevara evidently had a clear understanding of the relevance of Cuban agriculture to the effort underway to achieve basic industrialization of Cuba's economy. The Department of Industrialization, which he created under the umbrella of INRA, took a particular interest in the transformation of agriculture (and thereby agrarian reform) and was described as "one of three or four nerve centres of the revolutionary program" (Huberman & Sweezy 1960:129).

6. To overcome the negative economic impact of dependency — dependence on the export of raw materials and primary commodities in exchange for the import of manufactured goods from the centre of the world capitalist system — ECLAC (see Prebisch, 1950) prescribed a policy of "import substitution industrialization" (ISI) for Latin American countries on the periphery.

7. The "informal sector" refers to unregulated street employment as opposed to regulated work for wages or salaries in factories or offices. This informal sector tends to be occupied by rural migrants to cities who are forced into street employment due to the lack of paid jobs. Davis's "planet of slums" refers to the urban living conditions of these rural migrants.

8. Of course, it is evident and has to be acknowledged that this "agroecological revolution" was brought about not only by design and concern for ecological sustainability, but by circumstances. These circumstances were the sudden inability to access sources of oil, chemical fertilizers, pesticides and other inputs necessary for mechanized agricultural production and the inability to create conditions needed to fuel both industry, mechanized agriculture and sources of transportation. Under these crisis conditions, especially the lack of market access to oil and energy, productive capacity slowed and the output of the economy declined overall by 38 percent, one of the deepest crises of modern times.

9. <http://barbudosdesierramaestra.blogspot.mx/2014/04/nearly-66-thousand-women-join.html>

10. Agriculture was a centrepiece of the package of reforms implemented under the tenure of President Raúl Castro (see the discussion in Chapter Eight). These reforms included offering land in usufruct to any group of citizens wishing to farm it and the heavy promotion of the CCS cooperative sector (privately owned credit and service cooperatives). The reforms also included the "further decentralization of agriculture" by means of setting up networks of supply shops to sell farming inputs, which would improve farm gate and commodity prices paid by the state and thus raise the cap for bonuses above surplus production (Wright, 2009:243).

8. Updating the Model

1. The high level of social development is surprising because conventional development theory assumes and specifies a strong correlation between what economists call "economic growth'" (annual increase in the total output of goods and services) and the conditions of social development (education, health, housing, welfare, etc.).

2. In this period the Cuban government instituted a policy that resulted in a dual economy, one in which Cuban pesos were used as a medium of exchange and circulated, and another, mostly in the tourist sector, where all transactions were conducted in U.S. dollars. This allowed the government to generate reserves of a foreign currency (U.S. dollars) that it could use to pay for imports while at the same time insulating the domestic economy from the forces of the global market. It could set prices for services such as housing rents according to government policy (to limit rent to 10 percent of household income) rather than relying on the instability of supply and demand. This dual economy created enormous social problems (a waiter with access to dollars would have an effective purchasing power capacity that was up to ten times that of an urban professional such as a medical doctor, teacher or government employee). Only in the past few years has the government begun to phase out this policy, which itself has caused other problems.

3. The convertible peso, sometimes given as CUC$, was one of two official currencies in Cuba, the other being the peso. It had been in limited use since 1994, when it was treated as equivalent to the U.S. dollar. But on November 8, 2004, the U.S. dollar ceased to be accepted in Cuban retail outlets, leaving the convertible peso as the only currency in circulation in many Cuban businesses. The convertible peso was, by the pegged rate, the twelfth-highest-valued currency unit in the world and the highest valued "peso" unit. On October 22, 2013, it was announced that the currency was to be scrapped by gradually unifying it with the lower value Cuban peso.

4. Here Raúl once again seems to equate capitalism with the market, failing to distinguish clearly between them, raising questions that he does not answer and sowing seeds of confusion.

5. The Report at this point notes that "in Cuba, under socialism, there will never be space for 'shock therapies' that go against the neediest, who have traditionally been the staunchest supporters of the Revolution; [unlike] measures frequently applied on orders from the IMF and other international economic organizations to the detriment of third world peoples and, lately enforced in the highly developed nations where students' and workers' demonstrations are violently suppressed."

References

Araujo, M.F. (1976). "The Cuban School in the Countryside." *Prospects* 6, 1: 127–31.

August, Arnold (1999). *Democracy in Cuba and the 1997–98 Elections*. Havana: Editorial José Martí.

____ (2013). *Cuba and its Neighbours: Democracy in Motion*. Halifax: Fernwood Publishing.

Bardhan, Pranab (1997). *The Role of Governance in Economic Development*. Paris: OECD, Development Centre.

Bateman, Milford (2010). *Why Doesn't Microfinance Work? The Destructive Rise of Local Neoliberalism*. London: Zed Books.

Bernstein, Henry (2010). *Class Dynamics of Agrarian Change*. Halifax: Fernwood Publishing; Sterling, MA: Kumarian.

____ (2012). "Agriculture/Industry, Rural/Urban, Peasants/Workers: Some Reflections on Poverty, Persistence and Change." Paper for International Workshop on Poverty and Persistence of the Peasantry, El Colegio de Mexico, March 13–15.

Blum, Denise F. (2008). "Socialist Consciousness Raising and Cuba's School to the Countryside Program." *Anthropology and Education Quarterly* 39, 2 (June).

____ (2011). *Cuban Youth and Revolutionary Values: Educating the New Socialist Citizen*. Austin: University of Texas Press.

Brito, Ana (2014). "Os 85 mais ricos do mundo têm tanto como a metade mais pobre." *Economia*. <http://www.publico.pt/economia/noticia/os-85-mais-ricos-do-mundo-tem-tanto-como-a-metade-mais-pobre-1620364>.

Castro, Fidel (1971). Speech at a rally held at San Miguel commune, Pedro Aguirre department, Chile. *Prensa Latina,* November 29. Castro Speech Data Base, LANIC.

____ (1992). Message to UNCED (Rio de Janeiro), June 12, Havana Prensa Latina, Report No. FBIS-LAT-92-118-S (18/06/1992).

____ (2000). Speech at mass rally called by the Cuban youths, students and workers on the occasion of the International Labour Day at the Revolution Square, May 1.

Castro, Raúl (2008a). Speech as President of the State Council and the Council of Ministers, at Closing Session of the National Assembly of People's Power, Havana, February. Available online.

____ (2008b). Speech during the conclusion of the first Ordinary Session of the 7th legislature of the National Assembly of People's Power, July 11. <http://www.granma.cu/ingles /2008/julio/mar15/29na-raul-i.html>.

____ (2010). "Cuba Does Not Fear the Lies Nor Does It Bow to Pressure, Conditionings or Impositions." Closing session of the Ninth Congress of the Young Communist League, Havana, April 4.

____ (2011a). "Central Report to the Sixth Congress of the Communist Party of Cuba, April 16." *Cuba Debate*, February 9, 2014.

____ (2011b). Closing remarks by Raúl Castro Ruz, at the Sixth Party Congress.

____ (2013). "Cuban Parliament: Raúl Castro Tackles Economic Update." Radio Havana Cuba, July 8. <http://en.escambray.cu/2013/cuban-parliament-raul-castro-tackles-economic-update>.

Craig, D., and D. Porter (2006). *Development Beyond Neoliberalism? Governance, Poverty Reduction and Political Economy*. Abingdon, U.K.: Routledge.

Davis, Mike (2006). *Planet of Slums*. New York: Verso Books.

de Rivero, Oswaldo (2001). *The Myth of Development: The Non-Viable Economies of the 21st Century*. London: Zed.

Deneulin, S., and L. Shahani (eds.) (2009). *An Introduction to the Human Development and Capabilities Approach: Freedom and Agency*. London: Earthscan/IDRC.

Desai, Meghdad (2000). "Globalization: Neither Ideology Nor Utopia," *Cambridge Review of International Affairs* XI, 1 (Autumn–Winter).

Díaz Gonzalez, Beatriz (1992). "Cuba, modelo de desarrollo con equidad." *Sistemas políticos. Poder y sociedad. Estudios de caso en América Latina*. Caracas: Nueva Sociedad.

____ (1999). "Collectivisation of Cuban State Farms: A Case Study." In José Bell-Lara (eds.), *Cuba in the 1990s*. Havana: Editorial José Martí.

____ (2004). "The Transition to Sustainable Agriculture and Rural Development in Cuba." In José Bell Lara and Richard A. Dello Buono (eds.), *Cuba in the 21st Century: Realities and Perspectives*. Havana: Editorial José Martí.

Dilla Alfonso, Haroldo (1993). "Cuba: la crisis y la rearticulación del consenso político (notas para un debate socialista)." *Cuadernos de Nuestra América* 10, 10.

Dilla Alfonso, Haroldo, and Gerardo González Núñez (1997). "Participation and Development in Cuban Municipalities." In Michael Kaufman and Haroldo Dilla Alfonso (eds.), *Community Power and Grassroots Democracy: The Transformation of Social Life*. London: Zed Books.

Dilla Alfonso, Haroldo, and P. Oxhorn (2002). "The Virtues and Misfortunes of Civil Society in Cuba." *Latin American Perspectives* 29, 4: 11–30.

Durston, J. (2001). "Social Capital — Part of the Problem, Part of the Solution. Its Role in the Persistence and Overcoming of Poverty in Latin America and the Caribbean." ECLAC, Santiago de Chile, September 24–26.

ECLAC (Economic Commission for Latin America and the Caribbean) (1990). *Productive Transformation with Equity*. Santiago: ECLAC.

____ (2008). *Statistical Yearbook for Latin America and the Caribbean*. Santiago: ECLAC.

____ (2009). *Preliminary Overview of the Economies of Latin America and the Caribbean 2011*. Santiago: ECLAC.

____ (2010). *Time for Equality: Closing Gaps, Opening Trails*. Santiago, Chile: ECLAC.

Espina Prieto, Mayra Paula (2004). "Social Effects of Economic Adjustment: Equality, Inequality and Trends Towards greater Complexity in Cuba Society." In Jorgé Domínguez, et al., *The Cuban Economy at the Start of the Twenty-First Century*. Cambridge, MA: Harvard University Press.

____ (2005). "Poverty, Inequality and Development: The Role of the State in the Cuban Experience." In Alberto Cimadamore, Jorge Siqueira and Hartley Dean (eds.), *The Poverty of the State: Reconsidering the Role of the State in the Struggle Against Global Poverty*. Buenos Aires: CLACSO.

Foster, John Bellamy, Brett Clarke and Richard Yorke (2011). *The Ecological Rift*. New York: Monthly Review Press.

Fox, Michael, and Silvia Laindecker (2008). "Beyond Elections: Redefining Democracy in the Americas." Video. Oakland: PM Press. <http://www.beyondelections.com>.

Frank, Marc (2008). "Cuba Removes Wage Limits in Latest Reform." *Reuters*, April 10. <http://www.reuters.com/article/idU.S.N 1032792120080410>.

____ (2012). "Cuba Broadens Economic Reform Measures, Plans New Measures." Reuters, Havana, July 26. <reuters.com/article/2012/07/27/us-cuba-reform-idUSBRE86Q00B20120727>.

García Brigos, Jesús Pastor (2001). "People's Power in the Organization of the Cuban Socialist State." *Socialism and Democracy* 15, 1 (Spring–Summer): 113–36.

Garcia, Luis (2002). "Agroecological Education and Training." In Fernando Fuenes et al. (eds.), *Sustainable Agriculture and Resistance: Transforming Food Production in Cuba.* Oakland, CA: Food First Books.

Gray, Alexander, and Antoní Kapcia (2008). *The Changing Dynamic of Cuban Civil Society.* Gainesville: University Press of Florida.

Gray, Patricia (2002). *Latin America: Its Future in the Global Economy.* New York: Palgrave Macmillan.

Guevara, Ernesto "Che" (1965 [2005]). "Socialism and Man in Cuba." In D. Deutschmann (ed.), *The Che Guevara Reader.* New York: Ocean Press.

____ (2006). *El Gran Debate sobre la economía en Cuba.* Melbourne and New York: Ocean Press.

Guevara, Ernesto "Che," and Raúl Castro (1996). "La conquesta de la esperanza." Diarios inéditos de la guerilla cuba, Deciembre de 1965–Febrero de 1957. Havana: Casta Editorial.

Guzón, Ada (2003). "Potencialidades de los municipios cubanos para el desarrollo local." *Tesis de Maestría.* Havana, Junio.

Haq, Mahbub Ul (2000). *Reflections on Human Development.* New York: Oxford University Press.

Harnecker, Marta (1979). *Cuba: Dictatorship or Democracy?* Westport, CT: Lawrence Hill.

____ (2000). *La izquierda en el Umbral del Siglo XXI: Haciendo Posible lo Imposible.* Madrid: Siglo XXI.

____ (2010). "Latin America and Twenty-First Century Socialism." *Monthly Review* 62, 3 (July–August). <http://monthlyreview.org.2010/07/01/conclusion>.

Harris, James (1992). "Introduction." In Sandor Halebsky and John Kirk (eds.), *Cuba in Transition: Crisis and Transformation.* Boulder, CO: Westview Press.

Heller, Patrick (1999). *The Labour of Development: Workers and the Transformation of Capitalism in Kerala, India.* Ithaca, NY: Cornell University Press.

Horowitz, Irving (1977). "Institutionalization as Integration: The Cuban Revolution at Age Twenty." *Cuban Studies,* July.

Huberman, Leo, and Paul. M. Sweezy (1960). *Cuba: Anatomy of a Revolution.* New York: Monthly Review Press.

____ (1969). *Socialism in Cuba.* New York: Monthly Review Press.

Kay, Cristóbal (1988). "Cuban Economic Reforms and Collectivisation." *Third World Quarterly* 10, 3 (July): 1239–266.

Kellner, Douglas (1989). *Ernesto "Che" Guevara.* New York: Infobase-Chelsea House.

Kirk, John (2012). *José Martí: Mentor of the Cuban Revolution.* Halifax: Fernwood Publishing.

Kirk, John, and Michael Erisman (2009). *Cuban Medical Internationalism: Origins, Evolution and Goals.* New York: Palgrave Macmillan.

Levins, Richard (2008). *Talking About Trees.* New Delhi: Leftword Books.

Limia, Miguel (1997). "Sociedad civil y participación en Cuba." *Informe de Investigación.* Havana: Universidad de la Habana, Instituto de Filosofía, Octubre.

____ (1999). "Experiences and Perspectives of Socialism in Cuba: A Proposed Interpretation." *Informe de Investigación: Human Development in Kerala and Cuba.* Havana: Universidad de la Habana, Instituto de Filosofía.

____ (1999b). [An un-paginated working draft of a paper which Limia delivered at a research workshop in Havana and which circulated for discussion.] Contact the publisher for further information.

Lobe, Jim (2001). "Learn from Cuba, Says World Bank." *Inter Press Services*, April 30.

Lopez Vigil, Maria (1999). *Cuba: Neither Heaven Nor Hell*. Washington, DC: Epica Task Force.

Madea, Benjamin, and Peter Rosset (1994). *Greening of the Revolution: Cuba's Experiment with Organic Agriculture*. Melbourne: Ocean Press.

Mandel, Ernest (1967). *An Introduction to Marxist Economic Theory*. <http://www.marxists.org/archive/mandel/1967/intromet/index.htm>.

Marín-Dogan, Michelle (2008). "Civil Society: The Cuban Debate." In Alexander Gray and Antoní Kapcia (eds.), *The Changing Dynamic of Cuban Civil* Society. Gainesville: University Press of Florida.

Martínez, Osvaldo, et al. (1997). *Investigación sobre el desarrollo humano en Cuba 1996*. Havana: Caguayo.

Martínez Puentes, Silvia (2003). *Cuba, más allá de los sueños*. Havana: Editorial José Marti.

Marx, Karl (1967a). *Writings of the Young Marx on Philosophy and Society*. New York: Doubleday & Co.

Marx, Karl, and Frederik Engels (1967b). *The German Ideology*. Moscow: Progress Publishers.

MEDICC *Review* (2005), "Towards Health Equity in Cuba." VII, 9 (November–December). <http://www.medicc.org/publications/medicc_review/pdf-files/0905.pdf>.

Medin, Tzvi (1990). *Cuba: The Shaping of Revolutionary Consciousness*. Boulder CO: Lynn Rienner Publishers.

____ (1997). "Ideologia y conciencia social en la Revolución Cubana," E.A.I.L. 8, 1 (nero–junio). <http://www.tau.ac.il/eial/VIII_1/medin.htm>.

Mehrotra, Santosh (2000). "Human Development in Cuba: Growing Risk of Reversal." In Richard Jolly and Santosh Mehrotra *Development with a Human Face: Experiences in Social Achievement and Economic Growth*. Oxford: Oxford University Press.

Mesa-Lago, Carmelo (1993). "Social Security and Prospects for Equity in Latin America." *World Bank Discussion Paper* No. 140. Santiago: CIEDESS.

____ (2000). *Market, Socialist and Mixed Economies: Comparative Policy and Performance — Chile, Cuba and Costa Rica*. Baltimore: Johns Hopkins University Press.

Mesa-Lago, Carmelo, and Alejandro Vidal (2010). "The Impact of the Global Crisis on Cuba's Economy and Social Welfare." *Journal of Latin American Studies* 42: 689–717.

Miroswky, P., and D. Plehwe (2009). *The Road from Mont Pelerin: The Making of the Neoliberal Thought Collective*. Cambridge University Press.

Mitlin, Diana (1998). "The NGO Sector and its Role in Strengthening Civil Society and Securing Good Governance." In Armanda Bernard, Henry Helmich and Percy Lehning (eds.), *Civil Society and International Development*. Paris: OECD Development Centre.

Morales, Esteban (2010). "Corrupción: ¿La verdadera contrarevolución?" UNEAC, April 12. <http://www.uneac.org.cu/index.php?module=noticias &act= detalle&tipo=noticia &id=3123>.

Nerey, Boris, and Nivia Brismart (1999). "Estructura social y estructura salarial en Cuba. Encuentros y desencuentros." *Trabajo de Curso, Maestría en Sociología*. Havana: Universidad de la Habana.

Nieto, Marcos, and Ricardo Delgado (2002). "Cuban Agriculture and Food Security." In Fernando Fuenes et al. (eds.), *Sustainable Agriculture and Resistance: Transforming*

Food Production in Cuba. Oakland, CA: Food First Books.

Nova, Armando (2002). "Cuban Agriculture Before 1990." In Fernando Fuenes et al. *Sustainable Agriculture and Resistance: Transforming Food Production in Cuba.* Oakland, CA: Food First Books.

____ (2012). "Cuban Agriculture and the Current Economic Transformation Process." *From the Island: Providing Unique Perspectives of Events in Cuba* 9. Washington DC: Cuba Study Group.

Nuñez Sarmiento, Marta (2007). "A Gender Approach to an Impossible Transition." Presentation to IDS/mMetropolis Project, Saint Mary's University, Halifax, September 14.

Ocampo, J.A. (2005). "Más allá del Consenso de Washington: Una agenda de desarrollo para América Latina." *Serie Estudios y Perspectivas* 26, Naciónes Unidas-CEPAL México.

OECD (1997). *Final Report of the DAC Ad Hoc Working Group on Participatory Development and Good Governance.* Paris.

Oficina Nacional de Estadísticas (1998). *Anuario Estadístico de Cuba 1996.* Havana.

____ (2006). *Anuario Estadístico de Cuba 2006.* Havana.

Petras, James, and Henry Veltmeyer (2000). *The Dynamics of Social Change in Latin America.* International Political Economy Series. Basingstoke, U.K.: Macmillan.

Portuondo, José A. (1980). *Itineratio estético de la Revolución.* Havana: Editorial Letres Cubanas.

Prebisch, Raúl (1950). *The Development of Latin America and its Principal Problems.* New York: United Nations, Department of Economic Affairs.

Rao, V. (2002). *Community Driven Development: A Brief Review of the Research.* Washington, DC: World Bank.

Razeto, L. (1988). *Economía de solidaridad y mercado democratico* III. Santiago: Programa de Economía del Trabajo (PET).

____ (1993). *De la economia popular a la economia de solidaridad en un proyecto de desarrollo alternativo.* Santiago: Programa de Economía del Trabajo (PET).

Risco, Isaac (2013). "Cuba under Raúl Castro's Reforms." *Havana Times,* February.

Rodrik, Dani (2007). *One Economics, Many Recipes: Globalization, Institutions, and Economic Growth.* Princeton, NJ: Princeton University Press.

Roman, Peter (2003). *People's Power: Cuba's Experience with Representative Government.* Lanham, MD: Rowman & Littlefield Publishers.

Romard, Mathew (2014). "Bridging the Rift: The Cuban Revolution and the Agrarian Question in Marxism." MA thesis, Sociology Department, Acadia University, Wolfville, Nova Scotia.

Rondinelli, D.A., J. McCullough and W. Johnson (1989). "Analyzing Decentralization Policies in Developing Countries: A Political Economy Framework." *Development and Change* 20, 1: 57–87.

Rosendahl, M. (1997). *Inside the Revolution: Everyday Life in Socialist Cuba.* Ithaca: Cornell University Press.

Saez, Emmanuel (2013). "Striking It Richer: The Evolution of Top Incomes in the United States." *Real-World Economic Review* 65. <http://rwer.worldpress.com/2013/09/27/rwer-issue-65>.

Sandbrook, Richard, Marc Edelman, Patrick Heller, and Judith Teichman (2007). *Social Democracy in the Global Periphery: Origins, Challenges, and Prospects.* Cambridge. Cambridge University Press.

Saney, Isaac (2003). *Cuba: A Revolution in Motion.* Halifax: Fernwood Publishing; London: Zed Books.

_____ (2009). "Homeland of Humanity: Internationalism within the Cuban Revolution." *Latin American Perspectives* 36, 1 (164 January): 111–123.

Save the Children (2010). *State of the World's Mothers 2010.*

Schwartz, Joseph M. (2009). *The Future of Democratic Equality: Rebuilding Social Solidarity in a Fragmented America.* New York and London: Routledge.

Selee, Andrew, and Enrique Peruzzotti (eds.) (2009). *Participatory Innovation and Representative Democracy in Latin America.* Washington, DC: Woodrow Wilson Center Press.

Sen, Amartya (1989). "Development as Capability Expansion." *Journal of Development Expansion* 19: 41–58.

Sen, Gita, Aditi Iyer and Chandan Mukherjee (2009). "A Methodology to Analyse the Intersections of Social Inequalities in Health." *Journal of Human Development and Capabilities* 10, 3: 397–415.

Stiefel, Matthias, and Marshall Wolfe (1994). *A Voice for the Excluded: Popular Participation in Development: Utopia or Necessity?* London and Atlantic Highlands, NJ: Zed Books and UNRISD.

Stiglitz, Joseph E., and Narcis Serra (eds.) (2008). *The Washington Consensus Reconsidered: Towards a New Global Governance.* Initiatives for Policy Dialogue Series. Oxford: Oxford University Press.

Stricker, Pamela (2007). *Toward a Culture of Nature: Environmental Policy and Sustainable Development in Cuba.* Toronto, ON: Lexington Books.

Sweezy, Paul M. (1990). "Cuba: A Left U.S. View." *Monthly Review* 42, 4 (September).

Sweig, Julia (2007). "Fidel's Final Victory." *Foreign Affairs* January–February. <http://www.cfr.org/cuba/fidels-final-victory/p12362>.

Taylor, Henry Louis Jr. (2009). *Inside El Barrio: A Bottom-Up View of Neighbourhood Life in Castro's Cuba.* Sterling, MA: Kumarian Press.

Tharamangalam, Joseph (ed.) (2006). *Kerala: The Paradoxes of Public Action and Development.* Hyderabad: Orient Longman.

Thomas, Hugh (1971). *Cuba: Or, The Pursuit of Freedom.* London: Eyre & Spottiswoode.

Thresia, C.U. (2014). "Social Inequities and Exclusions in Kerala's 'Egalitarian' Development." *Monthly Review* 65, 9 (February).

UNDP (1993). *Human Development Report: People's Participation.* New York: Oxford University Press.

_____ (1996). *Investigación sobre el desarollo humano en Cuba 1996.* Havana: UNDP.

_____ (2003, 2009). *Human Development Report.* New York: UNDP.

_____ (2010). *Regional Human Development Report for Latin America and the Caribbean 2010.* New York: UNDP.

Uriarte, Meren (2008). "Rediscovering *Lo Local*: The Potential and the Limits of Local Development." In Alexander Gray and Antoní Kapcia (eds.), *The Changing Dynamic of Cuban Civil* Society. Gainesville: University Press of Florida.

Vazquez, A. (2007). "Desarrollo local, una estrategia para tiempos de crisis." <http://www.dete-alc.org/-%20archivos/biblio/104.pdf>.

Veltmeyer, Henry (2005). "The Dynamics of Land Occupation in Latin America." In Sam Moyo and Paris Yeros (eds.), *Reclaiming the Land: The Resurgence of Rural Movements in Africa, Asia, and Latin America.* London: Zed Books.

_____ (2007). *Illusions and Opportunities: Civil Society in the Quest for Social Change.* Halifax: Fernwood Publishing.

Williamson, John (1990). "What Washington Means by Policy Reform." *Latin American Adjustment: How Much Has Happened?* Washington, DC: International Economics Institute.

World Bank (1994). *Governance: The World Bank Experience.* Washington, DC: World Bank.

World Health Organization (2007). *Core Health Indicators for the Americas.* The WHOSIS DATABASE. Geneva: WHO.

Wright, Julia (2009). *Sustainable Agriculture and Food Security in an Era of Oil Scarcity.* London: Earthscan.

Yepe, Manuel E. (2008). "Cuba Reforms Its Food Production Process." Cuba News. <http://www.walterlippmann.com/docs2057.htmlhttp://www.walterlippmann.com/docs2057.html>.

Zimbalist, Andrew, and Claes Brundenius (1989). *The Cuban Economy. Measurement and Analysis of Socialist Performance.* Baltimore and London: The Johns Hopkins University Press.

Index